MY LIFE IN PICTURES

MY LIFE IN PICTURES
TED WILLIAMS
WITH DAVID PIETRUSZA

KINGSTON, NEW YORK

TOTAL Sports Illustrated

NEW YORK, NEW YORK

SPORTS ILLUSTRATED® and *Total*/SPORTS ILLUSTRATED
are trademarks of Time Inc.
Used under license.

A conscientious attempt has been made to contact proprietors of the
rights of every image used in this book. If through inadvertence the
publisher has failed to identify any holder of rights, forgiveness is
requested and corrected information will be entered in future printings.

For information about permission to reproduce selections
from this book, please write to:
Permissions
Total Sports Publishing
100 Enterprise Drive
Kingston, NY 12401
www.totalsportspublishing.com

BOOK DESIGN BY TODD RADOM

Library of Congress Catologing-in-Publication Data

Williams, Ted, 1918-
    Ted Williams: my life in pictures / Ted Williams with David Pietrusza
        p. cm.
    ISBN 1-930844-07-7
        1. Williams, Ted, 1918--Pictorial works. 2. Baseball players--United
States--Biography--Pictorial works. 3. Boston Red Sox (Baseball team)--Pictorial works.
    I. Pietrusza, David, 1949- II. Title.

GV865.W5 A3 2001
796.357'092—dc21
[B]
                                                                        2001023360

Printed in Canada

I guess things come full circle. In his introduction, my father writes about his father. Now I'm writing about mine.

Most people think of my father as The Splendid Splinter, the last major leaguer to hit .400 in a season, a hero in the Marine Corps. You might remember his last home run in his last at bat in Fenway Park in 1960. John Updike immortalized the moment in "Hub Fans Bid Kid Adieu."

I know all the stories, but they aren't part of my memory. I was born in 1968.

I love to listen to my father talk about hitting—how to stride into the ball, how to keep your hands back, how to handle the off-speed pitch. When he talks about hitting he is indeed the master. But he's taught me a lot more than about just hitting a baseball.

He's taught me that there's no substitute for hard work. That's what my father has always said is the key to becoming a great hitter. But he's taught me that it applies to all aspects of life.

I've seen my father work hard to battle back from a series of health problems. He didn't give up and he didn't count on others to help him. He fought back. He worked to get well, including a lot of time spent in therapy, and he worked to stay well. If something is worthwhile, you have to work for it.

He's taught me the value of strongly held opinions, but he's also taught me to base them on facts and experience. And if someone else has a different idea, he's taught me that I should keep an open mind because I just might learn something.

I've seen my father help people when there was nothing in it for him. He's shown me how passion can make you great—whether it's hitting a baseball, fishing for tarpon, or just being a human being.

I've seen how much he loves baseball. Baseball wasn't just a paycheck for my father. He voluntarily took the biggest pay cut in baseball his last season because he felt he had had a bad season the previous year, a season not up to his standards. Standards aren't any good unless you live up to them.

He loves baseball because it's a great game, with a great history, and because it offers such a great opportunity for kids, and because it's so much of what this country is supposed to be about.

I've learned a lot from my father. I've learned about friendship and passion and quality and achievement. Most of all, I've learned about love and caring, and sharing what's important in life.

Thanks, Dad.

John-Henry Williams
Hernando, Florida
February 2001

Pictures bring back a helluva lot of memories to people.

They sure do to me.

They say "a picture is worth a thousand words." I guess some folks would say that's a damn cliché. I guess it is. Hell, I know that. I didn't spend *all* my time in the batter's box. But *dammit* a lot of clichés are *true*. And this one certainly is.

I was kind of a shy kid. I've developed into a bit of a talker since then. Particularly on such subjects as how damn hard it is to hit the slider. Or the best places in the Keys to go after bonefish.

But I couldn't even begin to put together the words to tell you what even the *simplest* picture—even just a crappy little snapshot taken with one of those old Brownie cameras—can tell you.

The expression on my face in the pictures my dad took of me when I had that little Dutch boy haircut. Take a look at that. Boy, I couldn't *wait* to get long pants.

The exact cut of a Red Sox uniform. Oh, how that itchy flannel could get all bunched up. How it could get soaked in big splotches of sweat. Uncomfortable? Hell, yes!

My teammates. Geez, they were something. Look at the pictures. Look at their faces. Joe Cronin. That big Irish mug of his. A great manager. A wonderful friend. Jimmie Foxx. Muscles in his hair, is what Lefty Gomez said about him. Gomez might have been right. Grove—Lefty Grove. Boy, he was a competitor. Maybe he didn't know how to *lose*, but he knew how to *win*—and that's all *he* cared about. Maybe that's all he *should* have cared about. You can see it all in their faces. See it all in those pictures.

A lot of old friends are gone now. Geez, I miss them. And without the pictures my memory of them might start to blur a little bit. But if I open a book or a magazine or a photo album and look at those old black-and-whites suddenly those old, old memories are clear again. Clear as day. Clear as a damn fastball down the middle of the plate.

I can tell you *part* of the story of my life. I can tell you about hitting .400 or fishing in the Gulf of Mexico. But you see a lot more in a picture. Plus, well, the mind plays *tricks* on you. The memories change. Your attitudes change. People tell you so much about yourself, you start to half believe *what they read*, rather than *what you lived*. Happens even to a curmudgeon like me.

But pictures don't change. No, they *don't*. Leave 'em in a drawer for 30 years, take 'em out and they don't change in the meantime. They don't change to suit the times, or to fit somebody's attitude about what you're *supposed* to think. There's a truth in them, maybe not *all* the truth—but a good part of it.

That's why I wanted to do this book. I was just so eager, so damn antsy, to get it all down on paper. I wanted to take out the old pictures I had. Dust 'em off. I wanted to find some new ones too. I wanted to look 'em all over one more time and put down what I thought of those pictures. Tell you what they have meant to me.

So we gathered up as many old photos as we could. Gosh, there were a lot of them. A lot. One after another. We blocked out some time and spread those photos out on my kitchen table. I've got a big kitchen table, and we needed a *big* damned table for this job. We took a good, hard look at those pictures. Some of them really surprised the hell out of me. Gosh, they were wonderful. And I picked some others out from my albums. Things nobody's seen before.

I think we got a good mix. I picked out the best pictures and put down my recollections of what they meant. *Who* was in them. *What* they meant to me. *When* it all happened. *What* was going on at the time.

I wanted to tell you some things you didn't know about Teddy Ballgame. About just how wonderful it was fishing up on the Miramichi or down in the Keys. Or just about anywhere really. Gosh how I loved to fish.

I wanted to tell you a little about my kids—John-Henry, Bobby Jo, Claudia. Geez, they're great kids. About my life down here in Florida—and about the little museum I've got down here.

Maybe I'll even clear up some things you *thought* you knew. So even though the pictures *are* important, pay attention to my words, too.

I put some work into them, you know—and there won't be another book like this one.

Ted Williams
Hernando, Florida

My mother was named May Venzor Williams.

She bought me my first glove, a Bill Doak model. She was from El Paso. Mexican-French extraction, and basically her whole life was the Salvation Army. She'd be out night and day, saving souls from San Diego to Tijuana, selling the *War Cry*, playing the cornet in the Army band. A lot of times Danny and I would be waiting up past ten at night for either her or my father to come home—even when we were just little kids, not much bigger than we were in this picture.

My dad, Samuel Williams, was seven years older than my mother. He was from back East, from outside New York City, Westchester County. He met my Mom in Hawaii. He was *not* Salvation Army, and that caused a lot of problems between the two of them. He was a quiet man, a professional photographer, a Spanish-American War vet. I can't say we were very close. I loved him—but I can't say we were close. I was a lot closer to my mother. Always thought I had to do right by her.

This is the earliest I can go back, since I don't think they had sonograms back then. At least, not in San Diego. You can see my given name was Teddy. My father—who had been in the Spanish-American War—was a big fan of Teddy Roosevelt. I wasn't too crazy about being "Teddy"—except, of course, when I was "Teddy Ballgame," but that wasn't on this damn form—so I made a little alteration.

Myself, my mother, and my younger brother Danny.

Danny (right) was smarter than I was, but he always had problems. Physical problems. All sorts of problems. He had leukemia and that caused tremendous weakness in his bones. Once he tried to throw an orange. Crack. The bone in his arm snapped—just like that. And he was always in all sorts of scrapes. Never could respect authority.

In 1939 my mother and father got divorced. This is Dad with his second wife. Like I said my dad never was much of a baseball fan when I was kid, never took much interest in it at all. I had to learn how to play from people like Rod Luscomb over at the playground, but as I started to get famous my dad would take more of an interest. I was starting to hit and get my name in the paper, and he would buy me a steak, a half-pound steak, before I played my game that day. I guess he was looking to build me up.

Here he is looking at a newspaper article about me.

AS YOU CAN SEE I HAD THAT CRAPPY HAIRCUT FOR A WHILE. I DIDN'T WANT IT CUT THAT WAY, FOUGHT TO GET IT SHORTER. FOUGHT LIKE HELL. YOU KNOW WHY? IT GOT IN MY EYES WHEN I HIT. I NEVER DID LIKE ANY DISTRACTIONS WHEN I WAS SWINGING A BAT.

My boyhood home—although not when I lived in it—4121 Utah Street. It wasn't a big home at all, just a tiny little place, only cost about $4,000. And I have to admit it wasn't always kept up right, wasn't always cleaned properly. The Spreckles family, a big family out in San Diego, helped my mother get the house. We were supposed to pay them back, and we tried, but I don't think we ever did.

The best thing about it was location. A guy named Chick Rotert lived next door. A great guy. A former game warden. He taught me all about bass fishing, showed me pictures of where he'd been, where he'd fished, what he'd caught. Geez, I loved that. He even helped me buy my first reel, a little Pflueger-Akron. Cost $3.98.

And our house was only a block-and-a-half from the North Park playground—a great place to play ball.

My mother sold a lot of *War Crys* during her Salvation Army career. Here she is in the 1940s, selling some copies to Harley Knox, a local dairy farmer who had become Mayor of San Diego.

That's yours truly, Theodore Samuel Williams,

in the second row, fourth from the right. Buster Brown's schooldays is what you might call this one. It's my first-grade class. In school I really loved history. American history. World history. It didn't matter. I couldn't get enough of it. My second favorite subject was penmanship, which I must admit showed considerable foresight on my part.

The North Park playground, where I *worked* and *worked*, and *worked* at hitting when I was a kid.

My first game, though, would have had to be in grammar school, in the Garfield School playground. Then I was forever trying to get on the junior high school baseball team, the high school team. Then I would go and play pepper all afternoon with some older person that would come over and hit.

Even as a kid I hit a couple out of that North Park playground. I remember my first homer. I was 15, and it was to center—maybe 250 feet. Not more than 280 tops.

Of course, the place, the playground, was nothing special. Balls taped together with that black electrical tape. But I loved it. I couldn't get enough of the place. We'd play baseball. We'd play softball. We'd play a game called "Big League." We'd play that on the playground. Hit the ball over a certain pipe—home run! That was the most fun I ever had in my life.

I was always trying to see how I could get quicker because I heard a couple of guys at the ballpark when I was 12 years old, 13 years old, saying that kid has quick hands. I said, "Wait until he sees me next time." I picked up things like that, that registered with me, compliments only pushed me to improve.

The playground director was a fellow named Rod Luscomb. Lusk had pitched in the minors and was still pitching semi-pro ball on Sundays. He would throw me batting practice for an hour or more. Then I'd throw to him. I tagged after him, hung around that little playground, for a good seven years. A wonderful, wonderful man. I can't give him *enough* credit for making me a ballplayer. I wish every kid could have a coach like Rodney Luscomb.

I HIT A TON AT HOOVER HIGH—.586 IN MY JUNIOR YEAR, .403 MY SENIOR YEAR. THEY GAVE ME A SILVER STATUETTE FOR MY HITTING.

TED WILLIAMS

My coach at Hoover was a fellow named Wos Caldwell. He was another strong influence on me. A wonderful man. He later taught architecture in Florida, but, me, even years later, when I was with Boston, I always called him "coach."

Yes, Theodore Samuel Williams was once a pitcher. As a kid. In high school. That's not too surprising. I was skinnier than hell, and I didn't have any muscles. I was stringy.

But I was big, tall, and bigger kids usually end up pitching. I wasn't overly fast, but I had a pretty good little curve and I had a good screwball. And I could get it over. I pitched one game in the minors, in 1936. Didn't do too well. Pitched once with the Red Sox in 1940. Fared a little better.

It's tough to imagine me in any major league uniform but Boston's, but here I am in a Cards uniform. The Cardinals were the Hoover High team—they're *still* called the Cardinals. That's me at the center of the back row, and I was still pitching and playing right field. We won a big tournament—Governor Merriam was even there—up in Pomona when I three-hit San Diego High. Beat 'em 6-1, and struck out 13. Against Santa Monica I once struck out *23*—and *homered* in the same game.

One of the teams scouting me was the *real* Cardinals, the St. Louis Cardinals. I really liked their scout, Herb Bennyhoven. I even went to their tryout camp out in Fullerton. But they were really looking at Lou Novikoff—the Mad Russian. Boy, he could hit—but only in the minors, as it turned out

The Yankees and Tigers were also looking at me. The Detroit scout, a guy named Bill Krug, told my mother I was too frail to play baseball. It would kill me. Hell, I was 6'3" and 150 pounds. I could sort of see his point—*now*. Bill Essick, the Yankees scout, a good scout, offered my parents a little money, but not much.

Did you ever hear the story where the Yankee scout is writing Jake Ruppert? He writes a letter to Ruppert and he says, about this kid Ted Williams—he wrote this letter in 1935 or 1936—he said that he shows promise as a hitter but smart pitching will get him out. Well *bleep*, I'm *15 or 16* for *chrissake* and smart pitching will get me out? They ain't *got* smart pitching down here.

It turned out I didn't sign with any of the big league clubs.

Back in the '30s, we didn't have the big leagues in California. The American League, the National League, didn't go west of St. Louis. No major league ball on TV out west—or anywhere. Not much radio. We had the Pacific Coast League, and it was a good brand of ball. Good players. Decent salaries. If you couldn't be in the majors that was the place to be—and some players even *preferred* the PCL to the majors.

Anyway, San Diego didn't have a Coast League team until 1936. Bill Lane owned the Hollywood Stars and when he was going to have the rent doubled at his ballpark, he moved the club to San Diego. That was the Padres, and they were a good club. Bobby Doerr at second. Hit .342. Vince DiMaggio—he was in *left*—and Cedric Durst—*he* was in center—in the outfield. Durst had played with Babe Ruth. A real good hitting team. Not a bad team overall. Two real smart old pitchers on board, Frank Shellenback—our manager—and Herm Pillette. Finished second.

I was still in high school when their season opened, my senior year. But when I graduated all those major league clubs were looking at me. So were the Los Angeles Angels, another Coast League club. But their manager, Truck Hannah, really annoyed my father with his attitude.

Of course, the Padres were also interested. It never hurt to have a local boy on the roster. And my mother liked the idea of my not having to leave home, not having to travel to some outpost in the middle of nowhere, a thousand miles from home. If the Yankees had signed me there was no telling where they would send me. Binghamton probably. Same story with St. Louis.

So the Padres started to look better all the time. Plus Lane got a few politicians to work on my mother. Civic pride and all that. I signed with Bill Lane for $150 a month. My bonus? I signed late in June, but they paid me for the *entire* month. That was it.

My first at bat? I fanned—as a pinch hitter—against a Sacramento righthander named Cotton Pippen. It took me a while to get in the lineup. Hell, I was still only 17. Finished the season at .271 in 42 games. No homers, but eight doubles and two triples. Nothing great, but you've got to start somewhere. And I loved the road trips, train rides up and down the coast, into that wonderful scenery in the Pacific Northwest, going into Los Angeles. Geez, I loved it all.

I stayed on the Padres for the 1937 season. They had promised my mother that, promised her they wouldn't farm me out anywhere. We dropped down to third, but still had talent. Our catcher, a guy named George Detore led the league in hitting. Cedric Durst was back. Jimmy Reese replaced Doerr. On Opening Day I was 18. At one point early in the season I went 0 for 18. But I ended up at .291 with 28 homers and 98 RBIs. We swept Sacramento in the first round of the Shaughnessy Playoffs and nailed Portland in the finals for the league championship.

I was very lucky in San Diego—and with the Padres. Here I was 17 years old, best hitter in high school, and I'm learning how to hit and I'm getting better. Now I'm getting better competition because I'm getting in games and some of those little pitchers in the Coast League were pretty good and they knew how to pitch. So I was hitting pretty good and here is where being surrounded with older players helped me. The opposition pitchers, they were starting to slow up on me a lot, a little slow ball and I'd be out in front and hit a ground ball or something. I just wasn't waiting on the ball. So Herm Pillette, who pitched for the Detroit Tigers in the 1920s—he was on the Padres, he said, "What are they throwing you?"

I said, "Some little crappy curve ball."

He said, "Why don't you go up there and kind of lay for one of those, just kind of lay for it a little bit?"

Well, I did—and I got a line drive to right field. I said, "Hell, if this keeps up …"

Pillette got me *thinking* at a young age about having an idea of what the pitcher was throwing. Then once you hit one of them slow curves the pitchers say, "I can't do that any more." So you get the pitch *you* want. I could never forget what happened when it went right for me. Like for example, looking for the curve ball, here it comes. Bang!

I had a good ability to get the bat on the ball. Still, a ball that wasn't a strike, that didn't look good to me, I'd let it go.

In December 1937 Eddie Collins came out to San Diego. Eddie had been

a great player, a Hall of Fame second baseman, one of the greatest ever. Now he was general manager of the Boston Red Sox. He hadn't come out west to see me. He was looking at Bobby Doerr and an infielder named George "Foghorn" Myatt. Collins saw me hit batting practice. I was pitching batting practice and hitting a little bit. He saw me hit. He went into the clubhouse while we were still hitting. He said to Bill Lane, "You got to promise me one thing, you're going to let me have first option on that kid." Turned out he bought Doerr, but not Myatt. I guess he didn't like Myatt, and the Yankees ended up with him. But Collins did buy *me*.

Bill Lane got $35,000 plus two players, Dom D'Allesandro and Al Niemiec. Me, I got a chance to go to a mediocre club, a mediocre club that was as far from San Diego as you could get and still be on the North American continent. I wasn't crazy about it.

But then I met Collins. What a gentleman! Kind, decent, friendly. He told me the Red Sox were building. That Tom Yawkey's money could build a contender. He told me some of that money could be mine. I'd get $3,000 my first year with Boston and $4,500 the next. Now, I was getting only $200 a month in San Diego, and that was only for the baseball season.

All of a sudden Boston started to look much better.

One of the best players—the very best—that Eddie Collins got for Mr. Yawkey was Lefty Grove. Grove had been a great, great pitcher for Connie Mack and the A's. He still was with Boston. Grove pitched in my first major league game, you know. Red Ruffing beat him 2-0. That will tell you something about Grove's 1939 season. Best damn ERA in the league—and all he could manage was 15 wins. Boy, that would frustrate anyone—and if you know *anything* about Lefty Grove, you *know* how he felt about it. There's one more thing about Grove. The night he won his 300th game—that was in 1941 and he was just hanging on by then—they threw a big party for him. Gave him a picture of everyone who was there. Everybody was there—except me. And, oh, I caught hell for that. 'Ted Williams is no team player'—that's what they said. But, here's the true story. I didn't know about that party. I don't know why—just one of those things—but, boy, how those writers blew it out of proportion.

TED WILLIAMS

You can probably figure out all the stuff about hitting but are wondering about that ice cream remark. I didn't drink. Didn't smoke. But, oh, how I loved ice cream. Milk shakes. Malteds. You name 'em. I loved them all. Still do. The difference was then The Splendid Splinter needed to put *on* weight.

The Sox assigned me to the Minneapolis Millers in the American Association. Oh, Minnesota, Geez, I love Minnesota. Boy, it was beautiful. The American Association played a very similar brand of ball to the Coast League. Maybe a little lower. Good players though. Pee Wee Reese at Louisville. Eddie Joost at Kansas City. Wonderful shortstops. Whit Wyatt tore things up at Milwaukee. Two more great pitchers at Toledo—Al Benton and Dizzy Trout.

Still I wasn't happy to be there. I wanted to be in the majors. *Thought* I belonged there. *Knew* I'd be back with Boston, and *knew* for damn sure I could do the job.

Once I got used to being in the American Association, I started to hit, and I didn't stop hitting until the season ended. I won the American Association Triple Crown—.366, 43 homers, 143 RBIs. For good measure I led in runs scored, total bases, and walks. We were sort of a mediocre club, sixth place and just barely over .500, but we produced some decent ballplayers. Stan Spence. Jim Tabor. Broadway Charlie Wagner—he was my first roommate with the Red Sox. Roy Parmelee.

Now, it did not hurt at all that Nicollet Park—that's where the Millers played—was only 278 down the right field line. Not deep in the right field alley either. Did not hurt me offensively, or defensively, because that's where my manager put me—right field. But when the chips were down, it was 278 feet for *everyone*. And only *Teddy Ballgame* put up those numbers. Only Teddy Ballgame won the *Triple Crown*. And they couldn't ignore *that* in Boston.

By the way, when I was at Minneapolis—and when I was at San Diego—I wore number 19, *not* number 9. No particular reason I wore number 19 in both places. That was just the way it was.

My manager at Minneapolis was an old-time baseball man named Donie Bush. Won the National League pennant with Pittsburgh in 1927.

Now, having a manager like Bush could only help a young player who wanted to discipline himself regarding the strike zone. In five of Donie's first six seasons in pro ball he led his league in walks.

I kind of drove him crazy with some my antics in the outfield, but what a dear old man he was. And everybody just loved him. Just loved him. One time, I was down on things, and told him I was packing my truck and heading home to San Diego. Donie didn't blow up, didn't yell. All he said, very calmly, was "OK, Ted, I'll line up the transportation and when you've had a nice visit you can come back." I went back to my room, unpacked, and forgot about it.

After Donie gave up managing he scouted for the Red Sox. Scouted until he was 84. Was still scouting when he passed away.

They called Lefty O'Doul, "The Man in the Green Suit." Me, I was just green when this picture was taken. It's my first major league spring training camp. Sarasota, March 1938. Even getting there was tough. That spring there had been a big flood out in California. Bobby Doerr and I were going to meet in the Imperial Valley to ride together to Florida, but we couldn't even phone each other. He had to use some ham radio operators to get in touch with me.

I had to borrow $200 to make the trip east, and when I got to Florida I got into trouble right away. Some guy called me "busher" and told me to tuck my shirttail in. I sassed him back. Turned out it was Joe Cronin, our manager.

That wasn't the only trouble I had. Some of the veterans—Doc Cramer, Joe Vosmik, Ben Chapman, all good hitting outfielders—didn't want *me* around, didn't want competition around, really, and gave me a lot of lip.

About a week later the club was heading out for its first road trip, to Tampa. I was on the bus—to Daytona Beach, to the Red Sox minor league camp.

I wasn't happy about it. I wasn't happy about what Cramer and Vosmik and Chapman had said to me, how they treated me. "Tell them I'll be back," I told Johnny Orlando, "and tell them I'm going to wind up making more money in this bleepin' game than all three of them put together."

The next year, I caught a real bad cold driving to Sarasota—I always had respiratory problems—and was so sick I had to spend three days in New Orleans before I could drive on. Still, I was in a lot better situation than the year before. I had torn up the American Association in 1938. And in the offseason the Sox had traded their right fielder, Ben Chapman, to Cleveland. My only competition was a fellow named Red Nonnenkamp—lefthanded hitter. He'd been around for awhile, but never showed much. Right field was mine to lose.

I didn't.

When Tom Yawkey took over the Red Sox they were just God-awful.

They were still smelling up the joint from when they dumped Babe Ruth and all their other talent back in the '20s. You know, it was Eddie Collins who got Mr. Yawkey to buy the team in the first place. They had gone to the same prep school—Collins was a lot older—but still they were fellow alumni.

After Mr. Yawkey bought the club, he hired Collins to run the team for him. Eddie used Mr. Yawkey's money to buy some talent, a lot of talent actually, from other teams—guys like Lefty Grove, Joe Cronin, Rick Ferrell, Max Bishop, Bill Werber. Quality ballplayers.

But probably the best player he purchased was Jimmie Foxx. "The Beast." Boy, was he ever built. In the book I did a few years ago, *Ted Williams' Hit List*, I ranked the top 25 hitters. I put Foxx number three, right behind Ruth and Gehrig. Power? Unbelievable power! When he hit a ball it sounded like gunfire. My rookie year—1939—he hit 50 homers. He was starting to wind down, but he still hit 50 homers. And what homers! I saw him hit one in Cleveland one day that must have gone 500 feet. I hit behind him my first year.

Well, he was just a gem of a guy, Geez. He started as a catcher, yep, catcher, and he went from position to position. He weighed about 190. He could swish a bat, swish the bat like Mantle.

The late Bill Lane, veteran Pacific Coast League owner, plucked tall and gawky Theodore Williams out of San Diego High School before he was 18. Ted Williams was a pitcher and outfielder then, but the Padres signed him for his unusual power at the plate.

Boston Red Sox gave $25,000 and two players for Williams, and his mother got another $2500 for his signature.

Sent to Minneapolis, Williams topped American Association in hitting, runs-batted-in, home runs and runs scored.

COPR. 1939 BY NEA SERVICE, INC.
Williams, not yet 21, is a bit eccentric, but smart, and a student of baseball. He calls his shots at the plate . . . sings going after fly balls. He wore a necktie for the first time when Joe Cronin bought him one on the training trip. *NEXT: Eddie Miller.*

The press started to notice me even when I was a rookie.

Not everything said in this cartoon is accurate. But I can't complain about that part about Theodore Samuel Williams being "smart." They had to get *something* right.

Hell, I went to Herbert Hoover High, not San Diego High—and that's just the start of it. It's true, I *wanted* to play at San Diego High. San Diego High was a newer school than Hoover. San Diego High was the one in downtown San Diego, and there was a lot of black kids on that club. They were stronger, their football teams were bigger and stronger. We had a hell of a time beating them. Damn, I remember, I pitched so hard and swung so hard against them, and was so involved in the game. For Christ's sake, it was like playing a World Series or something. Boy oh boy, we used to bear down against San Diego High.

The boxscore for my first major league game—April 20, 1939 at Yankee Stadium. Ruffing struck me out the first time up. Next time up—in the fourth—I caught a hold of a fastball. Double off the right-center field wall.

try once again.

The box score:

BOSTON (A.)	ab.	r.	h.	po.	a.	e.		NEW YORK (A.)	ab.	r.	h.	po.	a.	e.
Cramer, cf	4	0	1	2	0	0		Crosetti, ss	4	0	0	0	0	0
Vosmik, lf	4	0	2	3	0	0		Rolfe, 3b	4	1	0	0	2	0
Foxx, 1b	4	0	0	5	0	1		Powell, lf	4	0	3	4	0	0
Cronin, ss	4	0	0	2	1	1		DiMaggio, cf	2	0	1	3	0	0
Tabor, 3b	4	0	1	0	1	0		Gehrig, 1b	4	0	0	6	0	1
Williams, rf	4	0	1	3	0	0		Dickey, c	3	1	2	7	0	0
Doerr, 2b	4	0	1	4	3	0		Gallagher, rf	3	0	0	3	0	0
Desautels, c	3	0	0	5	1	0		Gordon, 2b	3	0	1	4	3	0
aNon'nkamp	1	0	0	0	0	0		Ruffing, p	3	0	0	0	3	0
Grove, p	2	0	1	0	1	0								
bPeacock	1	0	0	0	0	0		Total	30	2	7	27	8	1
Total	35	0	7	24	7	2								

aBatted for Desautels in ninth.
bBatted for Grove in ninth.

Boston ....0 0 0 0 0 0 0 0 0—0
New York ....0 1 0 0 1 0 0 0 ..—2

Runs batted in—Dickey, Powell. Two-base hits—Williams, Dickey, Tabor, Vosmik. Three-base hit—Powell. Home run—Dickey. Double plays—Doerr, Cronin and Foxx; Doerr and Foxx. Left on bases—New York 6, Boston 9. Bases on balls—Off Grove 2, Ruffing 1. Struck Out—Grove 5, Ruffing 5. Umpires—Ormsby, Summers, Basil and Pipgras. Time of game—1:47.

TED WILLIAMS

Myself and Tom Yawkey, the Red Sox owner.

Mr. Yawkey knew how lucky he had been in life up to this date. He had been in baseball before, his uncle—a big lumberman—was part owner of the Detroit Tigers. When his uncle died he got 20 million bucks. Four days later he went out and bought the Red Sox for five or six million dollars. He was a real wonderful man.

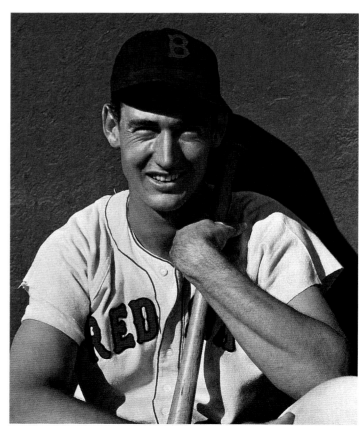

I remember talking to some of the old writers when I first came up. I said, "I don't see any blinding fastballs. I don't see any exploding curves." I expected to see a bigger difference between the majors and the minors. Sure, you saw some great ones in the majors, but overall there wasn't a big difference. I didn't feel bleepin' overwhelmed.

My rookie year. I've seen six or eight guys in my life that I thought absolutely had as much ability as I did. Still, they didn't do all that well.

Why not?

Intenseness. Those guys would see something *40 different times* and not get anything out of it. The next guy sees it in his own mind and uses it. That's the difference.

On a team flight with the Red Sox.

Boston wasn't the first big league team to fly—I think that honor went to the Reds when Larry MacPhail was running the club—but the Sox were *one* of the first. And that just goes to show how Mr. Yawkey took care care of his players, took care of his team. He loved the Red Sox, loved baseball, loved Fenway Park. Mr. Yawkey got rid of just about all the advertisements at Fenway, gave us a good green background to hit against. That was important—particularly if you're trying to hit .400. And he was always fair, more than fair at contract time. I just loved playing for him. You had to love playing for him

You might not know it (I don't know why you would) but I've always pretty much been a two-meal-a-day man—breakfast and supper. No lunch.

The other thing you might not know is this: That "Breakfast of Champions" slogan and I have something else in common besides this ad. It got its start in the Minneapolis Millers outfield—on a billboard on the fence at Nicollet Park—where I played in 1938.

After I signed my contract with Wheaties, I used to have a truckload of them going home each year. I used to get a carton of them when I hit a home run.

Well, *maybe* I was a little exuberant when I first came up.

I didn't express myself very well to the writers. I didn't go along with them quite as much as I should have. But it was just something that was not pre calculated or anything, it was just the way I was. I never said anything bad about anybody. That was never my style.

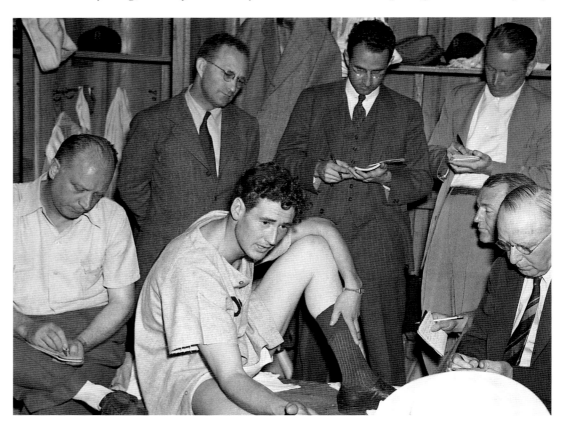

I was taking batting practice that day and I had fouled a couple and they went up in the screen behind me. You know what that tells me right away don't you? I was *just* a hair late.

Hugh Duffy was a coach when I first came up with Boston.

He used to tell me, "Son, you've got form and power. But the form is most important. With it you get the power. Don't monkey with your form." Duffy had been a big league outfielder back in the 19th century. Later, when the Sox were pretty bad, back in the 1920s, he managed them for a while. But the most important thing was that back in 1894 he had batted .440—no one's come close to that since. Not bad for someone 5'7."

I did pitch once in the majors. That was in 1940 when Joe Cronin put me in to mop up against Detroit. Two innings. Allowed three hits and one run. Struck out Rudy York on a big sidearm curve. It must have dropped about a foot. He always claimed I quick-pitched him.

Naah.

You know who Joe Cronin was? Joe Cronin was my first manager at Boston. Geez, Cronin must have thought I was a hell of a hitter to put me behind Jimmie Foxx.

He was another Californian, from up in San Francisco, like the DiMaggios. He'd started out with Washington, and married the owner's—Clark Griffith's—daughter. Then Griffith traded Cronin—his own son-in-law—to Boston.

I just loved Joe Cronin. He was a hell of a guy. Everything was happening in front of me, with me, and about me about that time. He was always trying to get somebody to say an encouraging word to me—and to get me out of the conflict I had all the time with the press.

Looking over wood at Hillerich & Bradsby, the bat people in Louisville.

There are a lot of stories told about how I cared for my bats, weighed them, knew if they were a little too heavy or a little too light—usually they'd get a little too heavy. They're pretty much true.

I *did* take care of my bats. Bone them down. Make sure they didn't take on extra weight. Hell, an extra half-ounce from dirt or moisture can make a big difference in your swing. How *fast* you get around. Where you make *contact*. Where the ball *goes*.

One of the great things about signing with San Diego was I also signed with Hillerich & Bradsby. Got a $15 check. Fifteen big ones. *Plus* I could order *all* the bats I wanted.

With Joe DiMaggio. People were always comparing us. We had those great seasons in 1941. We represented two of the greatest baseball cities in America—Boston and New York. It's true that we were once almost traded for each other. Del Webb had just bought the Yankees and he was toying with the idea of trading DiMaggio. Mr. Yawkey and he got as far as talking about it at Toots Shor's, but Mr. Yawkey wanted the Yankees to toss Yogi Berra—he was just a kid then, just barely out of the Navy—into the deal. Whether Yogi was the deal-breaker or not I don't know, but it never went through.

Berra was a wild swinger—but not *as* wild as people thought. He was a *selective* wild swinger. What do I mean by that? I mean he swung like hell at the *high* pitch out of the strike zone—but not the *low* pitch. Which actually wasn't too bad because he had the strength to hit that high pitch, strike or not.

I want to tell you about another little cigarette ad I did.

I never did smoke, but I had a great year, I don't know what year, 1940 or 1941. So they wrote me and said we'll give you $5,000 just to take some pictures. They hooked me into a room inside one

NAMED
THE PLAYER
OF THE YEAR
BY
The Sporting News
1949

"Smoke Chesterfield
...*much* Milder"
Ted Williams

Always **Buy** **CHESTERFIELD**

They're MILDER! *They're* TOPS! —{ WITH THE TOP MEN IN SPORTS / WITH THE HOLLYWOOD STARS / IN AMERICA'S COLLEGES

of the big buildings down there in New York, and there was a guy down there that had a special camera with a microphone right there.

So anyway, I did the ad. All I could think about was, Geez, they're going to give me $5,000 and it will take me a half hour up there. Then I thought, Geez, you may live to regret it if you don't do it. I could live a year on $5,000 then. So I decided I'd do it. Well, we did it and I always said I was going to give that money back to cancer research. I always said I was going to, but I never did.

I went into the 1941 All-Star Game hitting .405. So I went in pretty good—but I came out of a lot better.

The All-Star Game was in Detroit, at Briggs Stadium. The National League was holding a 5-2 lead going into the eighth inning. We cut that to 5-3 that inning.

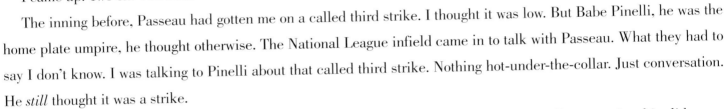

In the bottom of the ninth, Claude Passeau was on the mound. He got the first out, then Kenny Keltner reached on an infield hit. Then Joe Gordon singled. Then Passeau walked Cecil Travis—Travis was having a great year—to load the bases.

Joe DiMaggio came up next. Boy, the crowd was going crazy. Ninth inning. Bases loaded. DiMaggio. You couldn't beat it.

Joe hit a grounder, reached on a force. Damn near got doubled up, but Billy Herman's throw was wide. A run came in, so it was 5-4.

I came up. Two on. Two outs.

The inning before, Passeau had gotten me on a called third strike. I thought it was low. But Babe Pinelli, he was the home plate umpire, he thought otherwise. The National League infield came in to talk with Passeau. What they had to say I don't know. I was talking to Pinelli about that called third strike. Nothing hot-under-the-collar. Just conversation. He *still* thought it was a strike.

I swung at a couple of Passeau's pitches and, Geez, I was late, just a little bit late. His ball was coming, his slider was coming in on me. If it had stayed out there I would have been on it. But it was coming in on me. I didn't really realize what the ball was doing except, I said to myself, "I'm late on that ball, I'm a little late. I've got to quicken up." There was the next pitch right there, bang, and I hit it out. I wasn't sure it would make it. But it did. Third deck. Right field.

Three-run homer. I just scampered around those bases. I barely touched the ground.

The American League team was there to meet me at home. All of them. Bob Feller had already changed into street clothes. He rushed onto the field. Eddie Collins and Mr. Yawkey came out of the stands. Charlie Keller even *kissed* me. So did our manager, Detroit's Del Baker. *Kissed* me.

I stayed so long at the park after the game, I couldn't get a cab back to my hotel, the Hotel Cadillac. Finally, some guy gave me a ride. I asked him—and I asked his son who was in the car—if they knew about the American League winning.

They said no, they didn't really follow baseball.

At Yankee Stadium in May 1941.

Bill Dickey said I was absolute poison against New York that season. Said I hit some balls right out of his glove. Maybe I did. I hit .471 against the Yankees that year. I hit .485 against them at Fenway.

You know the story, probably, of how I was hitting just shy of .400 going into the last day of the 1941 season—I could have said I hit .400 by rounding the numbers up. I was hitting .3995 or something. But I didn't want to do it that way.

The last day of the year we had a doubleheader scheduled for Shibe Park in Philadelphia. I walked all around Philadelphia the night before with Johnny Orlando, our clubhouse man, my good friend, a wonderful man, and we were both wondering, "Am I going to be able to do it?"

Oh, Geez, we walked around for *four hours*, and finally I got back to the hotel, got up the next morning, and then when I got to the ballpark, Joe Cronin said "You don't have to be put in if you don't want to."

Well, God, that hit me *like a goddamn lightning bolt*! What do you mean I *don't* have to *play* today? He was going to let me sit it out for .400? He said, "You're officially .400." Anyway, I did play. I didn't want to hit .400 *that* way. My first time up I singled. The second time up, I homered to right. And then I got another line drive. Before I knew it, I had four hits the first game. In the second game I hit a line drive through the horns of the public address system in right field—the broadcasting horns. That went for a double, ground-rule double. I went 6 for 8 in the doubleheader and finished at .406.

But, you got to be lucky. *I know* you got to be lucky.

WILLIAMS OF RED SOX IS BEST HITTER

The most sensationally consistent hitter in big league baseball is a gangling, 22-year-old outfielder named Ted Williams of the Red Sox (*see front cover*). With most of the season behind him, Williams' hefty .400 plus average is almost certain insurance that he will ease into the American League batting title.

Williams is a great hitter for three reasons: eyes, wrists and forearms. He has what ballplayers call "camera eyes" which allow him to focus on a pitched ball as it zooms down its 60-ft. path from the pitcher's hand, accurately judge its intended path across the plate, and reach for it. He even claims he can see the ball and bat meet. The rest of his formula is never to stop swinging. On and off the field he constantly wields a bat to keep the spring in his powerful wrists. Even when he is in the outfield he sometimes keeps waving his arms in a batting arc. And, more than most other great batters, he keeps his body out of his swing, puts all his drive into his forearms.

Here on these pages are high-speed pictures taken by Gjon Mili which show the great co-ordination of these factors, the split-second release of power which enables Ted to hit safely four out of every ten times he comes to bat.

REPETITIVE-FLASH PICTURE SHOWS TED REACHING FOR A HIGH ONE, HITTING IT

① WAITING FOR BALL, WILLIAMS STANDS MOTIONLESS

② AS BALL NEARS PLATE, HE GETS READY FOR SWING

③ JUDGING PATH OF THE BALL, WILLIAMS CONNECTS

④ WILLIAMS KEEPS EYES FOCUSED ON THE HIT BALL

⑤ HIS POWER RELEASED, WILLIAMS FOLLOWS THROUGH

⑥ HE CLOSES EYES ONLY AFTER FINISHING THE SWING

CONTINUED ON NEXT PAGE 43

Life Magazine seemed to think I was a man to watch in 1941.

I got a chance to meet a lot of the other .400 hitters. I never did meet Joe Jackson, but aside from some of the 19th century guys, I met just about all of them—Cobb, Terry, Sisler, Hornsby, Duffy. This is Jesse "The Crab" Burkett. He hit .400 back-to-back, .409 in 1895 and .410 in 1896. He was just a little guy, but he could bunt like hell. That got his average up. One day, when he was past 70, he showed up at Fenway and after seeing how poorly the Sox all bunted, he took off his coat and said to the batting practice pitcher, "Put it over, as hard as you can."

He dropped a bunt right down the third base line, pretty as you could imagine it.

Then he did the same thing—down first.

Then he swung away—and lined one over second.

It's amazing what clean living can do for you.

Ruth was the home run king, but he was also the guy who did all the striking out. I wish I knew how to explain how Johnny Mize and Babe Ruth were so different. Because Mize didn't miss the ball. And Ruth—Geez, the strike-out king!

I never did talk hitting with Ruth. He wrote a book on hitting, and I had it once, but I don't know what I ever did with it. But the things he said in the book were right. He said things that I agreed with. But I'm the first guy who said I tried to get every ball in the air because I knew I got base hits in the air, home runs in the air—doubles, triples. I always wanted to hit the ball high.

I grew up hunting in San Diego, but I never saw *real* hunting until I got up to Minnesota. Boy, that was *the* place for duck hunting.

Myself and Joe and Dom DiMaggio.
I close my eyes, and I think about Joe DiMaggio, and all I can say is what a great player he was. He was as good looking a hitter as I ever saw. I keep going on and on about Joe DiMaggio because nobody ever had more admiration in their heart than I did for him. Of course, Dom belongs in the Hall of Fame as well. I don't know how they can keep him out. Wonderful defensive center fielder, .298 lifetime average, a good base stealer for his time.

They had a military draft even before Pearl Harbor, and they classified me 3-A—deferred because I was the sole support of my family. My mother and dad had divorced in 1939, and I was her sole support. I was also helping out my brother Danny. So 3-A was pretty normal, pretty standard procedure.

But not for *athletes*. When you're an athlete you become a *target*. Got a physical ailment that would ordinarily get you out? It *won't*. Not if you can throw a baseball or a left hook.

Over 30 and got six or seven kids? That won't get you out if you're *an athlete*, and the press starts *analyzing* your case. It'll get anyone else out—but not the athlete.

In January 1942 I was up in Minnesota. They sent me my notification; I was now 1-A—eligible for the draft. I thought that was wrong.

So I appealed, and it finally went to a Presidential Board. They did the right thing. Back to 3-A.

But, what a howl! You would have thought Teddy Ballgame bombed Pearl Harbor himself. Unpatriotic. Yellow. Those were the *milder* epithets. One Boston paper hired a private detective and sent him to San Diego to see if I was *really* supporting my mother. Of course, I was! Quaker Oats cancelled a $4,000 endorsement contract I had. Haven't eaten the damn stuff since.

Some people stood up for me. Will Harridge, the president of the American League, he was wonderful. Frank Graham, the New York sportswriter, he stood up for me. But there were some boos and some letters. I decided, *deferment* or not—*right* or not—and I *was* right—I had to sign up.

In May 1942 I went down to the naval recruiting station on Causeway Street. A lieutenant named Donahue swore me in, signed me up for naval aviation, gave me a second lieutenant's commission. I didn't have to report until season's end.

I reported for duty in November 1942. Went for ground school

training, at Amherst, Massachusetts—the Civilian Pilot Training Program at Amherst College. I had to take a cab to get there—and I was a day late—but I got there. The date was December 2, 1942.

I had some company at Amherst. My cadet class—which was only about 30 students—included Johnny Pesky, Joe Coleman, Johnny Sain, and another major leaguer—a guy you probably don't remember, a guy from the Braves named Buddy Gremp. We trained on Cubs, Piper Cubs, there. I almost wiped myself out one day on some power lines.

A lot of classroom stuff there—aerodynamics, navigation, you know. A bunch of guys washed out just from the coursework. The math scared me. Math was never my favorite. But I did a little prep work during the '42 season, before I went in, at Mechanics Arts High School. They had a preflight training program. Four hours a night. Three nights a week. Pesky was in on it, too.

One thing that slowed me down at Amherst was a damn hernia. They were driving us hard, on push-ups, sit-ups, swimming. Ended up spending two months at Chelsea Naval Hospital.

From Amherst I went to Chapel Hill, North Carolina—for preflight training. George Bush—he was then the Navy's youngest pilot, yeah, he became the youngest guy ever *shot down*—had training there the year before. Then on to Bunker Hill Naval Air Station at Kokomo, Indiana for basic flight training—100 hours of flight time. Man, there were a lot of planes there. Then to Pensacola for advanced training. My last training stop was Jacksonville, Florida for operational training. I learned how to fly both the SNJ and the F4U Corsair. Set a student gunnery record at Jacksonville.

Once you've finished operational training, you're ready for combat. I never got that far. I was in San Francisco on V-J Day. They sent me to Hawaii anyway—orders are orders, even if the damn war's *over*—but that was as close to the Empire of Japan as I got—in *that* war anyway.

They made a big thing out of my vision when I joined the Navy, really too big a thing.

Yes, I had good eyesight—20:10. They said I could read a baseball in motion or a record spinning around on a turntable. They said I could read the number on a license plate before somebody else could even see there *was* a license plate. That wasn't true. None of it. They said eyesight like mine occurred in only six out of every thousand people. Maybe that's true. I don't know. But I do know a lot of major leaguers have exceptional vision. An awful lot have 20:15 vision.

When I was kid, my right eye got hurt. Got hit with a hazelnut. Worried the *hell* out of me. I never had it checked, but, you know, sometimes it would bother me even when I was playing.

But all-in-all—yeah, I guess I *was* blessed with good vision. It didn't *hurt*. But that wasn't the key to hitting. The key was the right swing, studying the pitchers, studying the situations, waiting to get your pitch, and just plain *working like hell* at it.

Work, that's the real secret.

On the Navy team at Chapel Hill Preflight School. That's our coach, Lt. George Kepler. He was an officer in the V-5 program, former coach. Wonderful guy. And he worked with the cadets, getting them in shape. Whatever we were doing, he would be out there as part of the contingent that was working with us. Great fella. I got very friendly with him too.

I didn't play a whole hell of a lot of service ball, but I did play some. Johnny Pesky was on that Chapel Hill team. So were Harry Craft and Johnny Sain and Buddy Hassett.

I'm shaking Bobby Doerr's hand as I cross home plate in April 1946.

Of all my teammates, I was closest to Bobby Doerr. We were a lot alike. Both born in California—in 1918. We had played together on the Padres. We came up together. We liked the same things—movies, milk shakes, hunting, fishing. I even got to know his mother and father. They were wonderful people. I was so glad, so happy, when Bobby made the Hall of Fame in 1986. A lot of people think he was just a *hitter*. They forget what a wonderful second baseman he was as well.

The press was always around me. Always sniffing around. Trying to blow things out of proportion.

Could I have handled it smarter? Handled it better? I guess so. I was young then. I'm older now, smarter now, but you can be a thousand years old and still not know what to do about writers that are out to stir things up, to rip you.

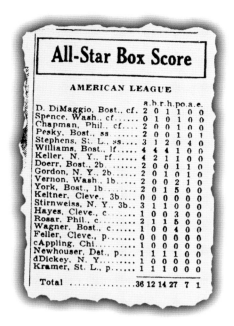

All-Star Box Score

AMERICAN LEAGUE

	a.	b.	r.	h.	po.	a.	e.
D. DiMaggio, Bost., cf.	2	0	1	1	0	0	
Spence, Wash., cf.	0	1	0	0	0	0	
Chapman, Phil., cf.	2	0	0	1	0	0	
Pesky, Bost., ss	2	0	0	1	0	1	
Stephens, St. L., ss	3	1	2	0	4	0	
Williams, Bost., lf	4	4	4	1	0	0	
Keller, N. Y., rf	4	2	1	1	0	0	
Doerr, Bost., 2b	2	0	0	1	1	0	
Gordon, N. Y., 2b	2	0	1	0	1	0	
Vernon, Wash., 1b	2	0	0	2	1	0	
York, Bost., 1b	2	0	1	5	0	0	
Keltner, Cleve., 3b	0	0	0	0	0	0	
Stirnweiss, N. Y., 3b	3	1	1	0	0	0	
Hayes, Cleve., c	1	0	0	3	0	0	
Rosar, Phil., c	2	1	1	5	0	0	
Wagner, Bost., c	1	0	0	4	0	0	
Feller, Cleve., p	0	0	0	0	0	0	
cAppling, Chi	1	0	0	0	0	0	
Newhouser, Det., p	1	1	1	1	0	0	
dDickey, N. Y.	1	0	0	0	0	0	
Kramer, St. L., p	1	1	1	0	0	0	
Total	36	12	14	27	7	1	

I hadn't played in an All-Star Game since 1942. A little thing called the war, you know. Actually, my 1946 game was a *helluva* lot bigger than my 1941 game.

The 1946 All-Star Game is known for my walloping that eephus pitch of Rip Sewell, but actually I was having a tremendous game even before that. In the first I faced Claude Passeau again. On a full count I walked. Then I scored, scored on Charlie Keller's homer. In the fourth I homered off Kirby Higbe into Fenway's center-field bleachers. Then I singled—again off Higbe—in the seventh. In the eighth I faced Ewell Blackwell—"The Whip." Fast. All arms and legs. Taller than me—6'6". Tough to follow. I singled off Phil Cavaretta's glove.

Then came the eighth inning, and Mr. Sewell. If you don't know what the eephus pitch was, let me tell you. Sewell developed it after he got hurt. Damn near got his foot blown off in a hunting accident. He would put a lot of backspin on the ball, almost like a damn shot put. It would fly up in the air—up, high up—a 25-foot arc. Looked like a pop fly. A lot of hitters were just too surprised to swing. And if you did hit it, well it wouldn't go anywhere. Wouldn't go anywhere because you had to supply your own power. Sewell never put a damn thing on it, that's for sure. Before the game I asked Sewell, "you're not going to throw that pitch to me, are you?" Sewell said he was.

Bill Dickey gave me some advice on how to hit it. He said the only way to generate enough power to hit it out was to get a little running jump on. Take a couple steps in toward Sewell. I fouled Sewell's first pitch back. I watched his second pitch go outside. His third pitch was a fastball—called strike two. Then came another eephus. I did just like Bill Dickey said. I slammed that piece of junk into the right-field bullpen—380 damned feet—for a three-run homer.

I set four All-Star records that day. Most RBIs in an game—5. Most runs scored in one game—4. Most RBIs, career—9. Most home runs, career—3.

By the way. Final score: American League 12, Nationals 0.

TED WILLIAMS

Writers were *one* thing—but you must admit I was accommodating to photographers.

That's me in the tarp.

Everybody was taking pictures back then because the 35 mm camera was just coming out, and every photographer had a 35 mm or two or three of them hanging on him. Cameras all over the joint and two or three photographers in every ballpark.

I got along decently with photographers. A friend of mine was Fred Kaplan. He did a lot of work for *Sport* and *Sports Illustrated*. One day he took his two-year old son, Lee, to Fenway Park. A few years later, Fred was going out to Fenway and the boy wanted to come along. Fred wanted to know why, who he wanted to see at the ballpark. "I want to see Teddy," Lee said.

"Teddy who?"

"Teddy Ballgame."

And that's how Theodore Samuel Williams became "Teddy Ballgame."

They brought all this stuff down from Gardner, Massachusetts in August 1946. At the time this chair was the world's biggest. Unless I hear otherwise, I will assume the bat *still* is the world's biggest. Over a thousand Royal Red Sox Rooters came down from Gardner—which was a big furniture town—to show their appreciation of the Sox. They ended up hauling the big chair back to Gardner, but if you go to Cooperstown you can still see that big bat. I preferred a 33-ounce model myself.

Liberty

OCT. 5, 1946   10c

Book:
CLEMENTINE
The funniest tale of
growing up since Penrod

**Here We Go Buying
Votes Again!**
BY HAROLD L.
ICKES

How the Red Sox Got That Way
BY DAVE EGAN

TED WILLIAMS

With Lou Boudreau in June 1948. I look a little wary. That's probably because it wasn't only in this picture that Lou was trying to take the bat out of my hands. Boudreau came up with that damn Williams Shift two years earlier.

After the 1946 All-Star Game, we played Cleveland at Fenway. In the opener of a doubleheader, I crushed the ball. Hit three homers, drove in eight runs. We won 11-10. In my first at bat in the second game I doubled down the line. Boudreau figured out that whatever he was doing against me wasn't working, so he tried something radical. The Shift. Boudreau—he was a shortstop—moved over to the second base side of the bag, playing a very deep second base basically. He moved second baseman Dutch Meyer to in back of him, back into the outfield. About 40 feet out of the infield. Kenny Keltner moved over from third base to just to the right of second. The outfield moved over too.

I had the whole left side of the field open. But I *didn't* give in, *wouldn't* give in, *wouldn't* give up my power game. They walked me a couple of times that game. My other times out I grounded out. And The Williams Shift pretty much became permanent, and I think, I *know*, it cost me points on my batting average.

But it didn't cost as much as you think. Right around the time Boudreau came up with The Shift, somebody was doing a study of where I hit the ball. Very early analytical stuff. What they found was only 10 percent of my hits were to left. Twenty-nine percent to center. Sixty percent to right.

Good enough. Sounds right. But there was more. Of my hits to left 60 percent were on the ground. Little dinky singles mostly. When I hit safely to center or right that fell to 28 percent. Seventy-two percent were in the air. Power hits. Doubles. Homers. So there wasn't *that* big a loss of hits, of productivity, because I wouldn't alter my swing. I still got my hits. Why should I have altered my swing—screwed up my swing *royally*—for a few lousy ground ball hits?

Ty Cobb couldn't figure that out. Babe Ruth could. He thought anyone who said I should hit to left was full of crap.

BOUDREAU SHIFT

SEEREY CF   EDWARDS RF

CASE LF

KELTNER 3B   CONWAY 2B

2B   BOUDREAU

WASDELL 1B

3B   1B

WILLIAMS

Mr. Yawkey had wanted a pennant for the longest time, had spent a helluva lot of money buying talent.

But he never got himself a pennant. We finally got one in 1946—Boston's first since 1918. Beat Detroit by 12 games—12 games—and they were a tough team, had Greenberg and Kell and Dick Wakefield and some fine pitchers: Newhouser, Trucks, Dizzy Trout. Yet we ran away from the league and got to face St. Louis in the World Series.

If there was a dynasty back then in the National League it was the Cardinals. Pennant after pennant. Musial. Schoendienst. Marty Marion. Whitey Kurowski. Enos Slaughter. Terry Moore. Just one great team, and that's the outfit we had to get past in the World Series.

it was no playful tap that York

Series Box Score

THIRD GAME
ST. LOUIS CARDINALS

	AB.	R.	H.	PO.	A.	E.
Schoendienst, 2b..	4	0	0	3	2	1
Moore, cf	4	0	0	3	2	1
Musial, 1b.........	3	0	1	8	1	0
Slaughter, rf.....	4	0	1	4	0	0
Kurowski, 3b.....	4	0	0	1	0	0
Garagiola, c.......	3	0	1	3	1	0
Walker, lf........	3	0	1	2	0	0
Marion, ss........	3	0	1	2	3	0
Dickson, p........	2	0	1	0	2	0
aSisler	1	0	0	0	0	0
Wilks, p...........	0	0	0	0	1	0
Total............	30	0	6	24	10	1

BOSTON RED SOX

	AB.	R.	H.	PO.	A.	E.
Moses, rf..........	3	0	0	2	0	0
Pesky, ss..........	4	1	2	1	3	0
DiMaggio, cf......	4	0	1	4	1	0
Williams, lf.......	3	1	1	2	0	0
York, 1b..........	4	2	2	12	0	0
Doerr, 2b.........	4	0	2	2	8	0
Higgins, 3b.......	3	0	0	1	0	0
H. Wagner, c.....	3	0	0	3	0	0
Ferriss, p.........	4	0	0	0	3	0
Total............	32	4	8	27	15	0

aBatted for Dickson in eighth.

St. Louis.........0 0 0 0 0 0 0 0 0—0
Boston ....3 0 0 0 0 0 0 1 .—4

Runs batted in—York 3.

Two-base hits—DiMaggio, Dickson, Doerr. Three-base hit—Musial. Home run—York. Stolen base—Musial. Sacrifice—H. Wagner. Double plays—DiMaggio and Pesky; Pesky, Doerr and York. Passed ball—Garagiola. Earned runs—St. Louis 0, Boston 3. Left on bases—St. Louis 4, Boston 8. Bases on balls—Off Ferriss 1 (Musial); Dickson 3 (Williams, Higgins, Moses). Struck out—By Dickson 4 (Doerr, Ferriss, Moses, Williams); Ferriss 2 (Moore, Slaughter).

Pitching summary—Off Dickson 6 hits, 3 runs in 7 innings; Wilks 2 hits, 1 run in 1. Losing pitcher—Dickson.

Umpires — Barlick (NL), plate; Berry (AL), 1b; Ballanfant (NL), 2b; Hubbard (AL), 3b. Time of game—1:54. Attendance—34,500.

The park is Sportsman's Park (you can tell by that ring around the mound). The batter is Theodore Samuel Williams and this picture illustrates what a Williams Shift looked like in practice. It didn't make much difference. I hit .383 against the Browns in the four years before there was a Williams Shift—.408 in the next six.

The bunt.

It's not like I had *never* bunted any other time, but you couldn't tell that from the coverage this bunt got then—and since for that matter.

It was during Game 3 of the 1946 World Series. I wasn't hitting good so I had the whole field. Eddie Dyer—the Cardinals manager—was using a modified Williams Shift, and the left side of the St. Louis infield was wide open—and all I could do was lay one down and see if it would be in play.

So in the third inning—Pesky had made the first out—I pushed a bunt down the third base side, pushed it all the way into left field, and reached first.

We won 4-0, went ahead in the Series two games-to-one, but one paper headlined

"Williams Bunts." Rudy York had homered in that game, but Red Smith wrote that my bunt was bigger than York's homer.

TED WILLIAMS

In spring training 1947 with Stan Musial. Nobody has any higher opinion of Musial than I do. I thought he was really some kind of hitter. We both won the MVP in 1946—so we've got a reason to smile.

At the 1960 World Series a woman came up to me and asked for an autograph. Turned out she was Stan's mother. I should have been asking for *her* autograph.

It's 1947 and I'm digging in against Bob Feller at Fenway. I have to rate Feller as one of the all-time greats. Fast, just deadly fast. Feller, Whitey Ford, Bob Lemon, Eddie Lopat, and Hoyt Wilhelm—the five toughest pitchers I ever faced. Feller and Lem were the only two real hard throwers and Feller was the faster—and when he lost the zip on his fastball he got by by *outsmarting* you. Ford, crafty as hell. Lopat, a junkballer. And Wilhelm. Well, Wilhelm was in a class by himself with that knuckleball.

TED WILLIAMS

It helps, yes, it does, to have decent hitters around you in the lineup. No matter how good you are, you need that help. When I first came up I had Foxx, Cronin, Vosmik, Cramer, Jimmy Tabor. They can't pitch around you with a lineup like that.

After the war, more talent. Bobby Doerr. Johnny Pesky. Junior Stephens—a *great* hitting shortstop. And these three guys. Sam Mele. Stan Spence. Dominic DiMaggio.

Mele. A good player, but a little horseplay we had got him shipped to Washington.

Stan Spence was a good player. As good as most of the crop of players that are playing today. He was a fairly big guy, a strong guy. He was a good lefthanded hitter. We played together in the minors. Then he came up to Boston and got traded to Washington—just like Mele. But we brought him back in 1948. Good extra-base power.

Dom DiMaggio. He had good speed, good arm. The press liked to make up stories that Dominic and I didn't get along. Crap. Total bleepin' crap. We're friends *to this day.*

I DON'T KNOW WHAT THE OCCASION OF THIS PICTURE IS—BUT I LIKE THE LOOKS OF IT.

Not even Mark McGwire bulks up *this* big.

Actually, it's some trick publicity shot they took in Sarasota in 1948—although, this *might* have been how Theodore S. Williams looked to some pitchers.

Joe Cronin replaced Eddie Collins as Red Sox GM after the 1947 season. Joe McCarthy came in to to replace Cronin on the field.

McCarthy was as good as they came. He'd never played major league ball—they called him a busher when he came up. But he had all kinds of major league experience. Managed the Cubs and the Yankees to pennants. When he took over the Yankees they were kind of faltering. Ruth was on the way out. DiMaggio hadn't arrived. McCarthy got them back on course. He really made the Yankees into a championship *machine*.

He left New York in the middle of the 1946 season, and was out of baseball in '47. He had a reputation as a taskmaster, a disciplinarian, a guy you didn't fool with. No-nonsense. All the writers said, "Oh, Terrible Teddy Ballgame's in for it now."

They asked McCarthy if he and I would be able to get along. He said "If I can't get along with a .400 hitter, it'll be *my* fault."

He had a rule on the Yankees. Suits and ties on the road. Suits and ties when you were with the team in the hotel dining room. I *never* wore ties. Hated them. It was strictly sports shirts for me.

In spring training, we all ate together in the dining room. I stayed up in my room. Ordered room service. But McCarthy went into the dining room. No tie. The biggest, loudest, damn sport shirt they made. End of *that* issue.

McCarthy was professional. A disciplinarian. But not heavy-handed. Fair. Not buddy-buddy. Not much small-talk with the players. It all came together with him.

We never won a pennant under McCarthy. Came close in '48. Came close in '49. It wasn't his fault. Just wasn't meant to be. We just ran into *very* slightly better teams.

I cried when they told me Joe McCarthy died.

TED WILLIAMS

We had a tremendous shot at the pennant in 1949, but the Yankees were just too damn tough for us. We went into the last two games of the season playing New York at Yankee Stadium. We just had to win one game, just one lousy, flippin' game.

This picture was taken in the first game after Johnny Lindell hit a homer in the eighth to sink us. Lindell was a punch-and-judy hitter, but he crushed one past me, right into the seats. Stengel should have pinch hit for Lindell. He had Gene Woodling on the bench. He had Charlie Keller on the bench. Good hitters. But he let Lindell hit, and he kills us. That's baseball.

The next day, we lose again. Lose the game. Lose the pennant. And I lost the batting race—and another Triple Crown. Boy, that was one tough series. One tough series.

TED WILLIAMS

In 1947 I won the Triple Crown. I didn't win MVP.

In 1948 I won the batting crown—hit .369, my highest since my .406 season—and led the league with 44 doubles, a .616 slugging percentage, 126 bases on balls, and a .497 on-base percentage. All in all, a decent year. A year a lot of folks would consider an MVP year.

I finished third that year to Joe DiMaggio. DiMaggio got 324 votes. Lou Boudreau got 213. I got 171. Joe had a quality year. I don't want to take anything away from him. He led the league in homers, total bases, RBIs. My complaint isn't with him—or with Boudreau. Lou Boudreau had one of the greatest years I've ever seen anyone have that year, both on the field and as a manager.

What *did* frost me—what *does* frost me to this day—is the bias of the writers. One of them—not from Boston, from the Midwest—left me off the ballot entirely. Bleepin' *entirely*! Not even a 10th-place vote. Not even the *courtesy* of that. Only three writers picked me for first.

Well, in 1949, I didn't lead the league in batting. I hit .3427, but George Kell hit .3429—*two tenth-thousandths higher*— so I lost out to him. It was a dogfight going into the last day of the season, but he went 2 for 3 against Cleveland. I went 0 for 2 against Vic Raschi. That really hurt, because I did lead the league with 43 homers and 159 RBIs. That was my all-time high in RBIs. My all-time high in homers. Still I missed the Triple Crown by an eyelash. And, of course, that last game of the 1949 season, that was the game in which the Yankees clinched the pennant over us.

So based on what happened in 1948 I wasn't too optimistic about winning the MVP award. Hell, based on *1941 and 1947* I wasn't too optimistic about winning. I hit .406 and didn't win. I won the Triple Crown and didn't win. What do you have to do to win an award in this league, to be *recognized* by the knights of the keyboard?

Well, they fooled me. In the off-season I went down to Arkansas, to the Superior National Forest, to do some fishing. For muskies. While I was there I got a call from my business manager Fred Corcoran. Fred gave me the news: I was American League Most Valuable Player. I got 13 first-place votes and didn't finish lower than fourth on any of the other writers' ballots. I won in a walk: 272 votes to Phil Rizzuto's 175.

TIME

THE WEEKLY NEWSMAGAZINE

Hy Peskin

TED WILLIAMS

Spring is busting out all over.

That's me with Connie Mack—"Mr. Mack" is what everybody called him. Everybody had the utmost respect for him.

He was just about at the end of his career when this was taken. He managed just about forever.

But what I remember most was meeting him when I was just a rookie, back in 1939.

Here I am, my first year in the big leagues, and I got some good players around me, Foxx, Tabor, Cronin, Cramer. I'm hitting behind Jimmie Foxx— me, a damn rookie! I never realized it then, what a load they're putting on me. I didn't think about that. As I looked back then I started to think, Geez, this is something, they're putting me behind Jimmie Foxx. I was hitting *better* than Foxx. I was hitting so well that Earle Mack, Connie Mack's son, said "Ted, meet me early at the ballpark, will you?" I said sure. He said, "I want my dad to meet you."

So I went to Shibe Park, and he had a little office that wasn't as big as my kitchen, a little loft up there. So I went up there and I meet Connie Mack. The only thing I really remember that he said to me, he had a real long, long turkey neck, thin, tall, and he said, someday you're going to become one of the greatest hitters. That's what he said to me.

You know, there would be a few things said early in my life like that, where I would say, "Geez, you must think I'm pretty good."

It was the same as when I was in the Pacific Coast League. I got a chance to talk to Lefty O'Doul. He damn near hit .400 one year. He was a hell of a hitter. I went up to him and he was taking a sunbath with a towel around him in the outfield. I told him who I was, I said, "I'm Ted Williams, I just signed with the Padres." He said, "I know who you are." Then I asked him a question, "What do I have to do to become a good hitter?"

Then he gave me the first line that lifted me up about five feet taller than I was. He said, "Kid, don't ever let anybody change you." At first I thought he was just trying to be nice. The more I thought about it though, the more I realized that what he said was the greatest compliment anyone could give me.

This picture is kind of ironic. It's myself and Ralph Kiner chatting before the start of the 1950 All-Star Game. The photographer probably snapped it because we were both great hitters—and both San Diego boys. It was what happened just after the game started that made the photo ironic.

People don't remember what a fine hitter Kiner was. I know he never hit much for average. Of course, he never had anyone in that Pittsburgh lineup to protect him. That—and a good eye for the strike zone—explains why he drew 100 or more walks six times. I never saw a more devastating righthand hitter. He was a much bigger guy than Jimmie Foxx. He had *long* arms, *big* arms.

In the very first inning of the 1950 All-Star Game Kiner hit a ball deep to left, near the scoreboard, way deep. I went back on it and crashed my elbow into the wall. Oh, how it hurt, but I didn't really know how much damage had been done. I had hurt it bad. Casey Stengel, the American League manager, he wanted to know if I wanted to come out, if I was all right. I wouldn't admit anything was wrong. I said I was fine, and even stayed around to put the AL ahead in the fifth with a single off Don Newcombe. After a really painful strikeout in the eighth—and I mean painful *physically*—I finally left the game.

Williams Makes Fine Catch

The National League's second batter, Kiner, slammed into one of Raschi's swift pitches and sent the ball riding toward the scoreboard in left center for what looked like an extra base hit. But Ted Williams, who some folks think specialize exclusively in getting his bat on a ball, got his glove on this one for a spectacular running catch that sent him careening off the wall.

For a moment it looked as if the Boston kid had hurt himself as his left elbow crashed into the barrier, but after some vigorous rubbing Ted signaled he was still sound in wind and limb.

Only three National Leaguers d Raschi in t peering round

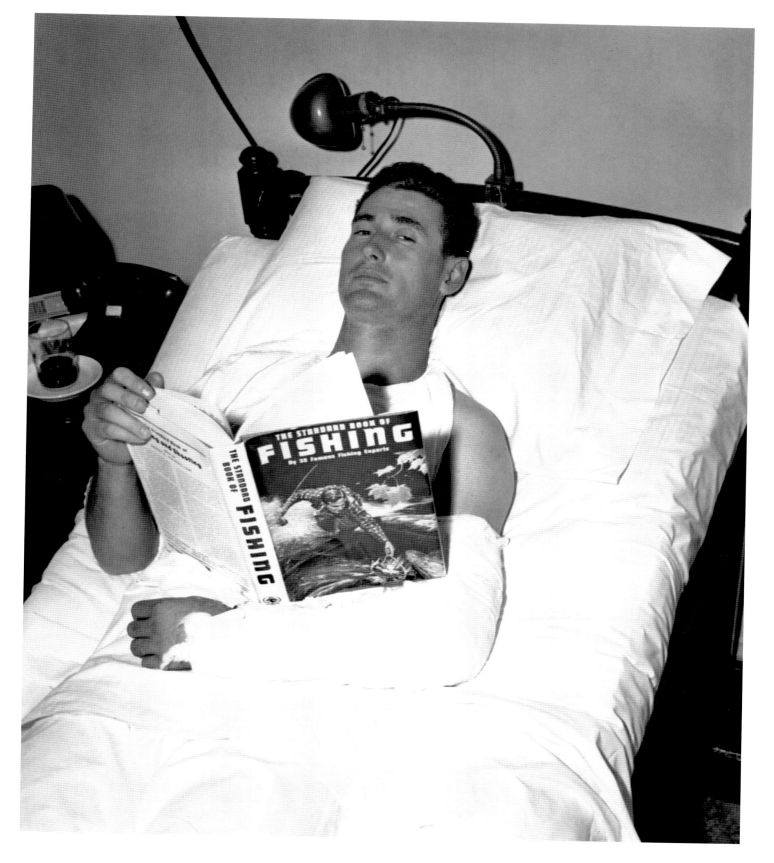

Recuperating in a Cambridge hospital just after my surgery.

I guess the reason I'm boning up on my fishing, is because at this point *nobody* really knew if I'd even play again. What a feeling. Oh, I came back. But I never really hit as well, certainly I never threw as well.

THIS IS FROM AN AD, BUT I ALWAYS DID ENJOY GOOD
FOOD AND WASN'T AVERSE AT ALL TO TRYING MY HAND
AT COOKING. NOTHING FANCY, NOTHING FANCY AT ALL
MIND YOU, JUST STEAKS AND FISH AND STUFF. BUT
WHAT I DID CAME OUT EDIBLE, IF I SAY SO MYSELF.
AT LEAST THERE WERE NO FATALITIES RECORDED.

Mickey Mantle was the greatest single ballplayer of all the athletes I've ever met. He was as down to earth as anyone, as sweet a guy. Never had a braggadocious vein in his body. He could do everything. Hit farther than anybody, switch hitter. But he thought everybody in the world was better than him.

Don't ever say Teddy Ballgame didn't hustle.

I'm trying to score from first on a double Clyde Vollmer banged off the left-field wall at Yankee Stadium. And come to think of it, the ball also bounced off Joe DiMaggio's chest. If it wasn't for Hank Bauer chasing the ball down in left I could have made it. Oh yeah, that's Yogi Berra putting the tag on me. We lost that day 5–1 to New York as the Yankees moved closer to the 1951 pennant.

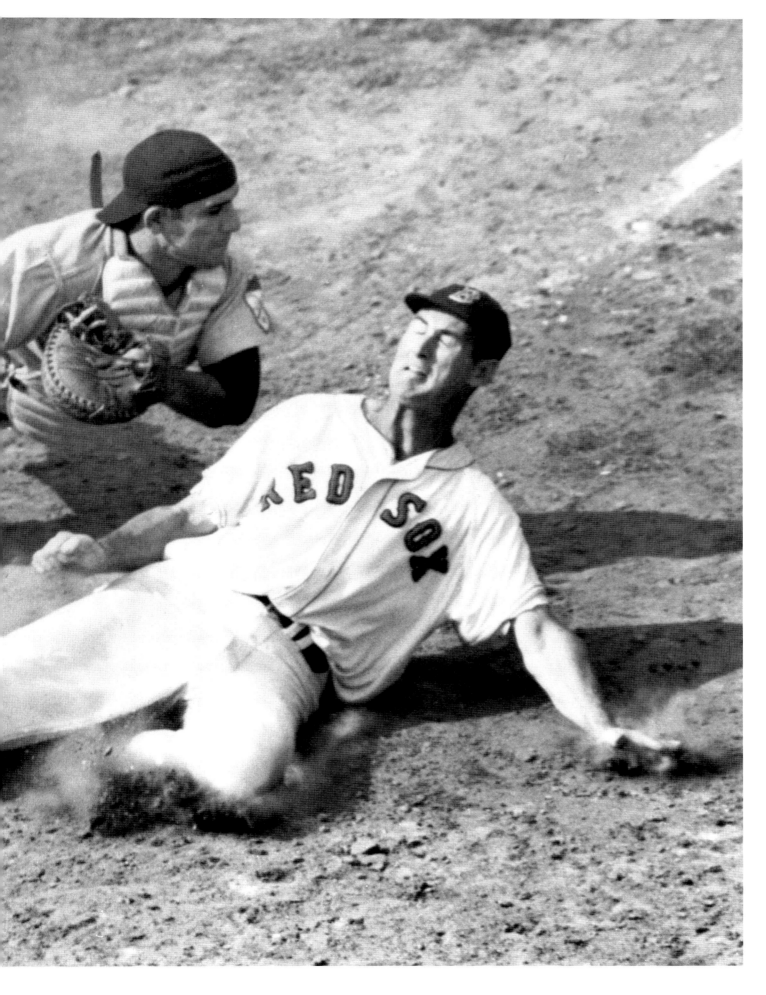

Jim Thorpe, that big old Indian. He was some nice guy. They'd taken all his

Olympic medals away from him and he had a second marriage, a little red headed girl, and he was a wonderful guy. He would come into the clubhouse early in the day and he'd sit in there in the restroom and we would talk.

So anyway, I was going to be at the Sportsman's Show in Boston with the Big Indian. We would go out on the stage together. He was a pretty good hitter you know, with the New York Giants, John McGraw's team.

He started talking to me one day when we were together in the clubhouse: "You know Ted, you ought to try to get along with these writers a little better. He said you know, they can"— I had heard this but it didn't sit good with me to hear it—"They can make you or break you." I didn't take to that. So we continued, and Thorpe says to me, "I used to have trouble that way too. They wrote stuff about me. I was playing for the Giants and I was hitting .324 or .328 or something, and they always said I couldn't hit."

He said this one writer wrote an awful bad article that said he didn't drive in many runs. It said the players on the club didn't particularly like him. And then it said he really isn't helping the club too much.

Then he said, "I talked to the guy, and I asked him what he would do if someone wrote something like that about him. The writer said 'I guess I'd punch him in the nose.'" He said he punched that writer right in the nose. Bang! He hit him in the nose and knocked him down. Bang, he knocks him down!

The Mighty Thorpe! A great guy.

Fenway did have some interesting visitors in May 1951.

We got 29 old timers in to help celebrate the 50th anniversary of the American League. Here I am with Cy Young—won more games than any other pitcher, 511. Ty Cobb was in town too. He thought I should have been hitting more to left. Hell, at that point I should have been hitting more *period*.

TED WILLIAMS

THIS WAS TAKEN IN 1951. MUST HAVE BEEN SPORTSWRITERS AROUND.

When Mayor John Hynes and the city of Boston proclaimed "Ted Williams Day" in April 1952, they promised me it would *not* be a big deal. I didn't want a big deal. So they told they've give me a watch—an aviator's watch—and give my daughter Bobby Jo a bike. That was supposed to be it. Well, it wasn't. One of the gifts they gave me was a memory book that 400,000 fans signed. They sang "Auld Lang Syne," and it was off to war—again.

Addressing the crowd at Ted Williams Day on April 30, 1952. That Korean War veteran alongside me—sitting in the wheelchair—Fred Wolfe. He kind of put things in perspective. You can lose a lot more than big league playing time in wartime. You can lose a *lot* more. The whole scene choked me up. That veteran. The crowd. I almost tipped my cap, but I didn't. I *did* tell the crowd—and it was a big crowd—"This is the greatest day of my life. I'll always remember it. It is a day every ballplayer looks for, and one I thought I'd never have. I never thought when I came to the Red Sox organization fourteen years ago that they were such a wonderful organization. They've been wonderful to me." I still feel that way.

They showered me with gifts, just *showered* me, including this Cadillac. A powder-blue Cadillac, damn it. Mayor Hynes gave me a silver bowl. My teammates gave me a motion picture projector. Well, I paid them back a little. In the seventh it was 3-3. Dominic DiMaggio was on first and I launched, just launched, one into the right-field bleachers, against Dizzy Trout. Final score: Sox 5, Tigers 3. We were in first place at the time.

When the U.S. went to war in Korea—and it was *the right thing* for us to do—I was in the Marine Corps Reserves. I loved to fly, oh, how I loved it, and staying in the reserves was a good way to stay in the air. In 1952 they started calling up reservists. Not all of them, but I was on their goddamn list. I was going on 34 years old. I had already served in World War II. I had banged the hell out of my elbow back in 1950. It was a mess. In other words, I didn't think it was fair, I didn't think it was *right*, to be called up again.

But there's always a tendency to pick on the athletes, to single them out, so I got called up again. I wasn't crazy about it, no way. In fact, deep down I was damn bitter about it—but I went, and I wasn't about to bellyache about it no matter how I felt.

Bob Kennedy and I were the only major leaguers to serve in both Korea and World War II. This was taken in Miami, after we got back from maneuvers at the Roosevelt Roads Naval Air Base in San Juan, Puerto Rico. We were both flying F9s. Both called up as captains in the Marine Reserves. Both major leaguers—he was an outfielder with Cleveland before he got called up.

Kennedy was a good pilot. But God, he went into the service and he had three or four kids. He married a girl that had a couple. Then they had a couple more. Geez, he was loaded with kids. Finally, they decided they didn't want him, because he had too many dependents.

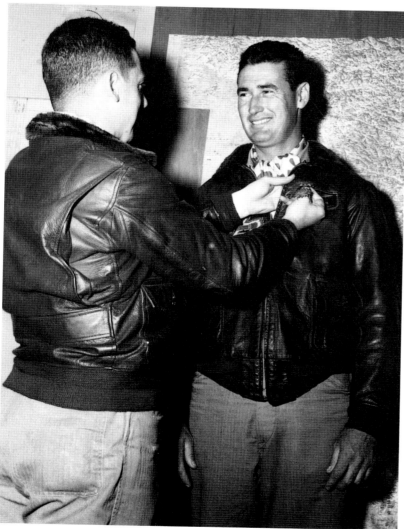

In my Corsair at Cherry Point, North Carolina— September 1952.

RECEIVING MY WINGS. IF YOU DON'T THINK THAT IS A HELLUVA MOMENT, A MOMENT TO BE PROUD OF, WELL, I DON'T KNOW WHAT I CAN TELL YOU.

TED WILLIAMS

Well, I suppose you want to know about the crash landing.

I was flying a mission—a big mission—in North Korea, pretty deep into the country. To a place called Kyomipo. It was near Pyongyang, the North Koreans' capital. We must have had 200 planes just bombing the hell out of them. Bombing troops, dropping anti-personnel weapons, flying pretty damn low. *Had to*, to hit our targets with any accuracy.

I was so low, I got hit with small arms fire. That was all, but it hit my hydraulic lines and was enough to set off every damn light on my control panel like it was a bleepin' pinball machine. The plane started shaking, heaving. I could barely control the stick.

Serious? Damn straight it was *serious*.

I tried to radio for help. But no answer. Then up came a plane behind me. Lt. Larry Hawkins was the pilot. He wanted me to eject, pop right out. I couldn't hear him. But if I had I don't think I would have. Those cockpits were so damn small—and I was so goddamn big—if I had blown out of that plane, I would have left my knees behind.

It's funny. I should have been thinking of *nothing* but saving my Marine hide, but even then, even then, I was thinking baseball. No knees. No baseball.

Meanwhile, Hawkins is trying like hell to tell me something. He's telling me my plane is on fire. And he's telling me to *rise*—to get higher—because when your aircraft is on fire that's what you do so you can then glide safely down.

Bailing out was now starting to look *good* to me. But Hawkins guided me out toward the Yellow Sea, then back to land, down to another airfield. Not the one I had taken off from, another one, closer to the action, closer to the front.

Oh God, there were dozens of planes trying to land, trying desperately to land. And then—Blam!! A wheel door explodes, blows right off. Should have taken the damn wing right along with it. Didn't. I'll never know why, but it didn't.

So I'm coming down, and I'm coming down at 225 bleepin' miles per hour—twice what I'm supposed to be doing. I hit the ground and skidded faster than hell. There was nothing to slow me down, and I skidded for 2,000 feet. Almost hit a couple of fire trucks. I was shouting, shouting at God, to get me home safe.

Man, I didn't know why it all didn't explode. When it finally stopped, I couldn't get out of the plane. Finally, I did, dove right to the ground, and I was so mad that I flung my helmet right down. They got me out of there quick, and it's a good thing. That plane caught fire and there was nothing left of it but a blackened hunk of junk. Had to haul it off the field with a crane.

They don't like to put pilots right back into the air after a close call like I had after bombing Kyomipo. They like to give you two or three days off, to settle down. But they were short of men, so I went up again—went up the next day. Over Seoul. A couple of months later I was flying over a place called Chinnampo. That was over on the west coast of the peninsula. I get hit *again*—antiaircraft fire this time—but this wasn't as bad as before.

All the while I was sick. Damn respiratory problems. Coughing like hell. Pneumonia. They put me in the hospital, flew me there, offshore near Pohang. Oh, I was sick. Had to feed me intravenously. I hated those tubes. And my inner ear—I couldn't hear the plane's radio—even when no Commie had shot my plane full of holes.

So in June they sent me back to Honolulu, said that was the best place to treat my ear. On the way, I made the mistake of talking to the press again. Popped off on the war. It didn't make any sense how we were fighting—that's what I said, and I was right. We weren't trying to win that damn thing. Forgotten War? Forgotten soldiers? That was us.

Anyway, the next month—July 1953—it finally occurred to them, that a nearly- deaf, pneumonia-prone, 34-year old pilot with a bum elbow maybe *wasn't* combat material. They mustered me out of the Marines, and I headed home.

TED WILLIAMS

I've been associated with the Jimmy
Fund since the late '40s. A great, great charity—
helping sick kids in Boston. Frankie Fontaine—"Crazy Guggenheim" from
the old Jackie Gleason Show—he was about the earliest booster it had.
Then Mr. Yawkey and the Red Sox got involved.

I never wanted any publicity about going to the hospitals. A lot of athletes do that—and publicity is not why they go. Seeing those kids just rips
your heart out. So many sad stories. It's the least you can do.

Batting practice at Fenway in July 1953. I was just back from Korea.

TED WILLIAMS

I hadn't intended to play at all in 1953. I was sick. I was tired. Hell, I had spent a little time at Bethesda when I got back. I needed to recuperate.

But it was the All-Star Break, and Ford Frick, the Commissioner, asked me to throw out the first ball at the All-Star Game in Cincinnati. Well, I went, and those people out there, they gave me a wonderful, wonderful ovation. Now, my agent, my good friend, Fred Corcoran wanted me to get back in the saddle. Wanted me to start playing. Branch Rickey—he was at the All-Star Game—he was working on me, wanted me to suit up again. A lot of people did. But it was that crowd that clinched it. No boos. Cheers everywhere. Wonderful. Just what I needed.

So I went up to Boston, to Tom Yawkey's office, and signed a contract to play the rest of the season. That day I went out to the field, took a look at home plate, and it didn't look right. I told Joe Cronin, it was off, out of line by, oh, maybe less than an inch. I don't think he believed me. But he figured he'd humor Theodore Samuel Williams.

Sure enough, it *was* off.

I took about a week to get into shape, get my legs limber, take BP—hit some shots off of Lou Boudreau, our new manager, I'll tell you. I got into a game on August 6. Made an out. But three days later I pinch hit a homer off Mike Garcia into the right-field seats—420 feet. On August 16, I was in the starting lineup for the first time. That was at Fenway. Twenty-five-thousand fans, and they gave a five-minute standing ovation, and I homered and singled.

I hit like hell the rest of the way—the greatest power tear of my career. Thirteen homers in 91 at bats. Get out the calculator! What's that? That's one homer for every seven at bats. I hit .407, slugged .901.

Nine-oh-one.

I thought I'd spell that out in case you thought it was a misprint.

Not bad for an old Marine.

Fishing for bonefish in 1953. I released just about every one I ever caught. Sometimes a bonefish will look a little lifeless once you've netted him. After you remove the hook, you take him and place him just below the surface of the water. Then move him back and forth under the surface. Get some water back into his gills. Keep at it if he doesn't seem to be responding right away. Why is this important? Because if you let him go and he's still out of it, still stunned, still winded, he's easy picking for a shark or a barracuda.

With Jean and Tom Yawkey and Lou Boudreau, who was our manager, in 1952. Boudreau replaced Steve O'Neill after the 1951 season. I got along decently with Boudreau. He never did win with the Sox, though, and when Mr. Yawkey decided to let Boudreau go, he asked me if I wanted to manage. No, thanks, is all I had to say.

HOW TO HIT .400? IT'S VERY SIMPLE— JUST GET FOUR HITS IN EVERY TEN AT BATS. I DON'T KNOW WHY MORE PEOPLE DON'T FOLLOW MY ADVICE.

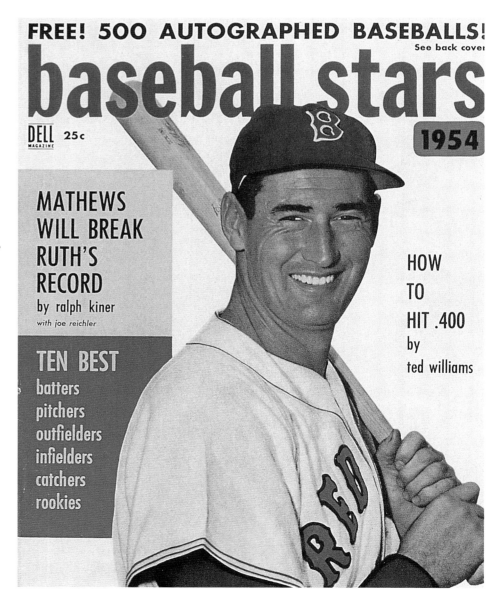

FREE! 500 AUTOGRAPHED BASEBALLS!
See back cover

baseball stars

DELL 25c
MAGAZINE

1954

MATHEWS WILL BREAK RUTH'S RECORD
by ralph kiner
with joe reichler

TEN BEST
batters
pitchers
outfielders
infielders
catchers
rookies

HOW TO HIT .400
by ted williams

That there is a real fisherman's prize catch. At the time I caught that fish, it was the eighth largest black marlin ever caught; 1235 pounds; 13-plus feet long. And that was what got me started to really try to conquer the world with a rod and reel.

As the 1950s wore on, I was just plain wearing out. I kept hitting, but I suffered one damn injury after another. Colds. Even ptomaine poisoning. I had to keep at it, to keep loose, keep limber, keep from pulling another damn muscle. But the real reason I wanted to show you this picture was the little fellow in the doorway—Johnny Orlando, the Sox trainer. He was one of my closest friends on the team—right from the very first spring training. He lent me five bucks to catch the bus to the minor league camp. He was my friend that day—and from then on.

Spring training in Sarasota in 1956. We started out in fourth and ended in fourth. We had some talent. I hit .345, second to Mickey Mantle's .353. Jackie Jensen. Mickey Vernon. Jimmy Piersall. Billy Klaus. They were decent, but overall we were basically just a mediocre team.

Spring training and I did not always get along.

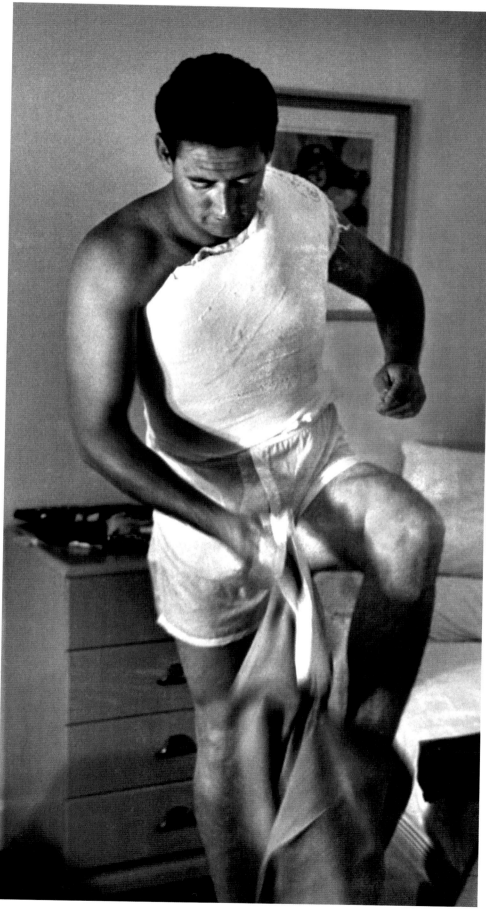

On the very first day of spring training 1954, I was playing the outfield, just shagging flies, and chatting—quite amiably—with our center fielder Jimmy Piersall.

Hoot Evers—he was one of our outfielders—was batting. He hit a liner toward left-center. I went toward it, bent down, then tumbled over, ass-over-elbows. I knew right away what happened. I could hear my collarbone go POP. Just like that.

"I broke it," I told Piersall, "I'm sure something's broken."

The damnedest thing is I had ridden up from the Keys, with a friend of mine, an orthopedic surgeon named Russell Sullivan. Sullivan operated on me a week later up in Boston. Took out a piece of bone an inch-and-a-half long. Put in a metal pin four inches long.

I'd like to say I returned to the lineup in 1954 with an immediate, dramatic, crash-boom bang. I'd like to say it, but it wouldn't be true. I pinch hit in a game on May 5, 1954 and flied out. I stayed in the game and grounded to short. Not very impressive, not very impressive at all, dammit.

But the *next* day we were scheduled for a doubleheader against Detroit. My collarbone still hurt like hell. I couldn't even sleep on my left side because of the pain. But I batted nine times and got eight hits, including two homers and a double—and I drove in seven. My second homer landed in the Navin Field upper deck. I was back—but the Red Sox weren't. They still lost 7-6 and 9-8. For the year the club was pretty crappy, 69-and-85, for a fourth-place finish—42, yes 42, games back.

For the year I managed to get into 117 games and led the league with a .635 slugging percentage, a .516 on-base percentage, and 136 walks. I paid a price for those walks. I batted .345 but had only 386 official plate appearances. I'll give Lou Boudreau, my manager, credit. He batted me second to try to get me more at bats. But it was no use. Cleveland's Bobby Avila, a good-hitting second baseman, hit .341, had the necessary "official" at bats, and was awarded the batting crown.

On the other hand, the people at *Total Baseball* have come up with a bunch of new statistics since then, and by their calculations I led the league in Total Average (1.452), Production (1.151), Adjusted Production (193), Batter Runs (70.9), and Adjusted Batter Runs (57.9). I like the way those guys think—even if it takes a degree from MIT to explain what most of those numbers mean. Production, though is pretty easy to figure out. It's a the addition of on-base and slugging averages—OPS they call it now. Even a Hoover High graduate can calculate that one.

Kneeling on deck in 1955. The people at *Sports Illustrated*—which was in its second year— liked the picture so much they put it on their cover.

1956. Nothing unusual here at all. Just the Kid talking hitting.

yself, Yogi Berra and Mickey Mantle in Washington for the 1956 All-Star Game. I went 1 for 4, but in the seventh I homered off Warren Spahn into the right-center-field bullpen. Mantle came up next, and he homered into the left-center-field bleachers.

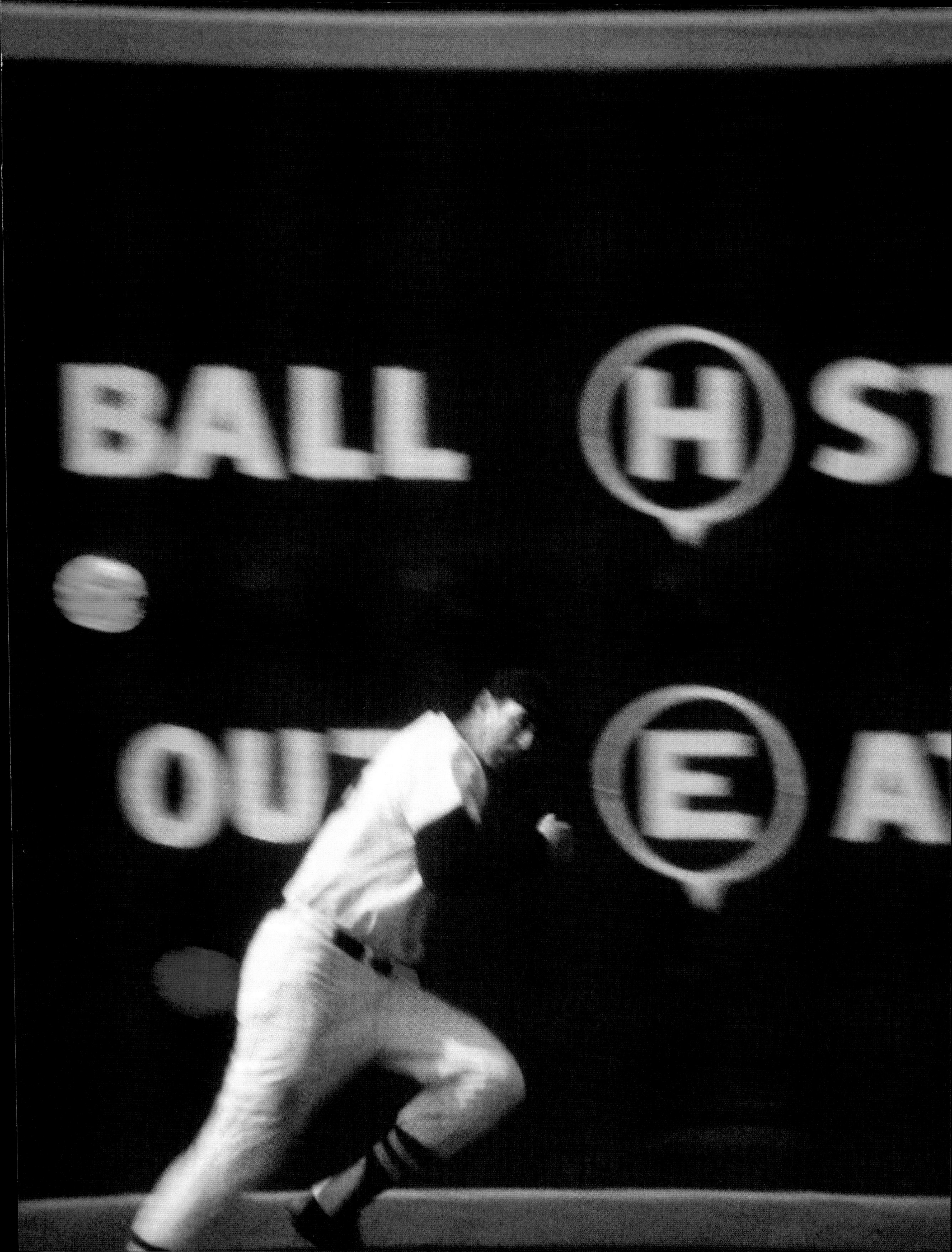
BALL
H
E

If I look a little under the weather in this picture—I probably *was*. I've always been susceptible to infections, to viruses, to respiratory problems. In Boston. In Korea. Even back when I was home in San Diego.

The Splendid Spitter. Great Expectorations. Yeah, the head-
line writers had a ball. We were at Fenway and playing the Yankees. It was tied nothing-nothing

going into the ninth. In the top of the ninth, Mantle hit a pop fly into the outfield—in back of the shortstop, in front of me.

I raced in for it, and it popped out of my glove. Oh, how those fans booed. I was mad at *myself*—and I was mad at *them*.

Then I made a nice catch of a ball Yogi Berra hit. Good over-the-shoulder catch. Cheers.

Cheers! One minute they booed the *crap* out of me. The next minute I'm a bleepin' *hero*! Lord, how Theodore Samuel Williams *hates* frontrunners. And that's what that crowd was in that inning—frontrunners!

Oh, how that ticked me off. So as I ran in, I spit. I spit to right field. Then I spit toward left field. And when I got to the dugout I didn't stop. I spat in the dugout, and for good measure I came out of the dugout—and spat *again*.

By now the crowd was going wild, and *I* wasn't about to calm down either. I got a walk with the bases loaded to win the game. But I wanted to *hit*, dammit! I was so mad I flung my bat straight up in the air.

Well, this *upset* people. It certainly upset Mr. Yawkey. He fined me $5,000—although I never really did pay it.

The next night we were playing Baltimore. Big crowd. Huge crowd. Everyone expected the crowd to *boo the living crap* out of me. I expected it too.

But they cheered. Gave me a tremendous ovation. Geez, I couldn't believe it. That got to me. These were wonderful fans. The best.

I homered in the ninth inning. Won the game. And as I rounded the bases, I cupped my hand over my mouth.

They *loved* it.

I am *not* doing a victory dance. This happened in September 1958, and I am bleepin' upset, oh so bleepin' upset because a terrible thing happened. I didn't mean for it to happen. It was an accident, pure and simple.

We were at Fenway, playing Washington. I was in a slump. With two on, I struck out looking. I was mad at myself, kicked the dirt, threw my bat down in disgust, but that stickum on the bat got caught on my hands and the bat went *up* not *down*—up into the stands. Seventy-five feet high—where it conked a woman, a 60-year-old woman named Gladys Heffernan, right in the head. Turned out it was Joe Cronin's housekeeper. I had never met her, but it didn't really matter who it was. That was purely an accident. I was upset. But she wasn't hurt seriously, and she was *so* gracious, so *nice* about it. I ended up getting her a $500 diamond watch for Christmas.

Oh, by the way, in my next at bat—same game—I tried to make it up to the crowd. Doubled to center to drive in an insurance run. Then I hit .500 for the rest of the season—14-for-28 and 7-for-my-last-11.

At an All-Star Game with Musial and Willie Mays.

In *Ted Williams' Hit List* I ranked Willie as the 10th best hitter of all time. Here's why. Great statistics. Great power, 660 homers—more than Foxx. Wonderful speed. Eleven Gold Gloves—well, that doesn't count toward his hitting—but it doesn't hurt to give the man credit. A wild swinger, but he had the power to make even a bad pitch take off. You really had to *see* him play to appreciate him fully. Just spectacular.

A pretty exclusive club—the .400 club—Bill Terry, myself, Rogers Hornsby, George Sisler.

Some sports writers said the Babe was my boyhood idol. That wasn't true. I used to read more about Bill Terry and Mel Ott than I did about Babe Ruth. Bill Terry was one of the greatest hitters that ever lived and certainly he captured my attention.

Rogers Hornsby I first met when I was at Minneapolis. I'd pick his brain, and I'd watch him hit. He was damn near 50 then but he'd still take his swings. And he could still whistle those lines drives into the outfield. Bang. Bang. Bang. Tough guy. No diplomat, but he told me one of the best things I ever heard: "Get a good ball to hit. You got to get a good ball to hit."

George Sisler I didn't know that well. He could have been as great as Terry or Hornsby, but his eyesight went down the drain right at his prime. Sinuses.

Sam Snead and myself, at a Sportsman's Show. I have a lot of respect for Sam and for golfers in general. But let me tell you, there is no comparison between hitting a baseball and hitting a golf ball, Oh, I know, Sam used to say, "Ted, in golf you've got to play your fouls."

Well, yeah, but *those* fouls aren't going 80, 90 miles an hour, aren't curving, aren't changing speeds. And *forget* about *knuckleballs*! There's no crowd in golf *yelling* at you, *booing* you. They're quieter than the crowd in church when the collection basket starts coming around.

In golf you get to practice, practice, *practice* your swing. Hundreds of practice shots a day. Most major leaguers are lucky to get 15 swings a day.

You can play damn near forever in golf. I finished up playing baseball when I was 42. That was considered remarkable back then—and for baseball, despite all the advances in training and medicine and surgery, it's still pretty damn rare. In golf I'd just be getting up a head of steam.

And, of course, in golf there aren't *nine* guys out there trying to take the bread out of your mouth.

No, golf's a fine sport, a fine *relaxation*, compared to hitting a baseball.

My first child, Barbara Joyce—Bobby Jo we call her, was born on Wednesday, January 27, 1948. She was premature—by several weeks, by several weeks dammit—and I was down in Florida fishing. Oh how the Boston press howled about that. Howled. And Paul Gallico of the *New York Daily News* chimed in. It got so bad that even Dave Egan had enough. "This is all an attempt to put Williams in the grease," he wrote. And he was right.

The date is August 1, 1957, and I'm batting against the Tigers. I started that year thinking it would be my last. And what happened in spring training didn't help matters any. A New Orleans sportswriter put into print some casual remarks I had made about Johnny Podres—the Brooklyn pitcher—being called into the service. It wasn't an interview. Just some talk over beers at an airport. But I said some things about the draft—and politicians, *mostly* about politicians—and about the Marine Corps. The next day I followed that up with some choice words about Joe Louis, a wonderful fighter. The IRS was hounding him over back taxes. It made my blood boil.

Still I had a great year, a wonderful year. My highest batting average—.388—next to my .406 year. Led the league in slugging percentage—.731. In on-base percentage—.528. Finished second in homers, with 38. Set a major league record with 33 intentional walks. Twice I hit three homers in one game, against the White Sox and against the Indians. Both times on the road. That game in Cleveland, I wanted to come out after my second homer. It was a cold, crummy night. But Pinky Higgins, my manager, talked me into staying in the game. I got homer number three and a place in the record books.

That September I homered in four consecutive at bats. I took me four separate games to do it, but I did it anyway. And off four decent pitchers— Tom Morgan of Kansas City. Whitey Ford—that was my only homer against him. Bob Turley—a grand slam. The last was off Tom Sturdivant. Sandwiched around that streak I had *another* streak. I reached base 16 straight times. Mickey Mantle edged me out for MVP, but *The Sporting News* named me Major League Player of the Year.

Not bad for someone who turned 39 that August 30.

Actually getting old *helped* me. My bat speed slowed down a little bit. Not all the time, but enough for me to occasionally hit the ball to *left*. So they started laying off that Williams Shift stuff, and when I *did* hit the ball to right, there were more holes for it to land in.

You don't always have to put up a sign this big to get my attention—but it helps. They had another one, too, calling me "the greatest American since George Washington."

This was taken on August 18, 1958 at Fenway. It took me awhile—it took me *too* long—to realize how much the Boston fans loved me, how they were the most loyal fans in baseball. It really came to me after that spitting incident in 1956. The writers thought that the fans would roast the hell out of me after that. They wrote that. They hoped it. But the fans crossed them up. They cheered me. The greatest ovation I ever got.

They won me over that night. The proved themselves the greatest fans in baseball. Not frontrunners. Fans.

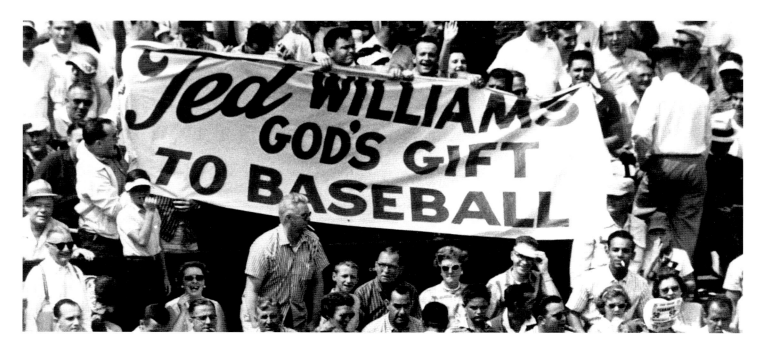

They put me on the cover *The Sporting News Guide* in 1958, and, if The Kid says so himself: it was not a bad choice at all. I had my last good year, my last great year really, despite starting the year with ptomaine poisoning—from bad oysters—and following *that* up by hurting my ankle, pulling a muscle in my side, and banging up my wrist a couple of times. Oh yes, and I turned 40 that August. Try having a good year under those conditions. I can assure that—at least in baseball—life does *not* bleepin' begin at 40.

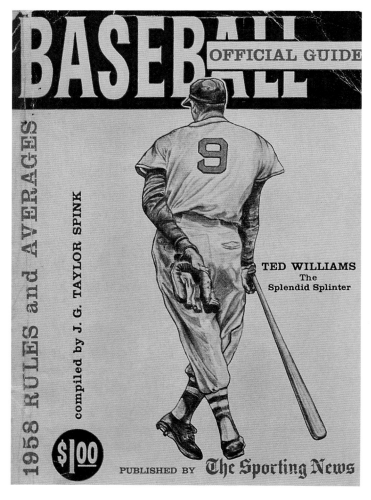

COMISKEY PARK NIGHT GAME. IT PAYS TO KEEP YOUR EYE ON THE PITCHER. DUR- ING WARM-UPS. WHEN HE'S PITCHING TO OTHER BATTERS. WHENEVER. KEEP YOUR EYES OPEN. YOU MAY LEARN SOMETHING.

TED WILLIAMS

In 1958 when I won my last batting crown I edged out this fellow—Pete Runnels. We were teammates. He had come in from Washington over the winter.

To tell you the truth I was pulling for Runnels. I had five—six, if you count the one I had in Minneapolis—batting crowns going into the season. Runnels didn't have much power. He needed more meat on his bones. But he *could* put the bat on the ball and slap it through the hole. He could put together a good year, but then he'd slump. For Runnels 1958 was a *good* year. From July on we battled Harvey Kuenn for the league lead. Like I say, I wouldn't have minded if Runnels had won. But I wasn't about to *give* it to him. I couldn't do that. Baseball isn't *charity*.

Late in September I caught fire. Nine-for-13. Two days to go and we're tied at .322. We go into Washington. In one inning we hit back-to-back-homers, but I went 3 for 3. He only went 2 for 3—although it took a helluva catch by Roy Sievers to keep him getting another homer and matching me hit-for-hit.

I was up by a little bit, but I still wasn't too confident. Pedro Ramos was pitching the last game of the season for Washington. Always tough on me. *Always.* First inning, though—Bam! Into the left-field bullpen. I got a double later in the game, Runnels went 0-for-4.

Teddy Ballgame: .328. Pete Runnels: .322.

I am happy to say, though, that Runnels finally got his batting championship—in 1960, my last year with the Sox, when he hit .320.

Pepper to me is just great. Absolutely wonderful for improving your coordination whether you're trying to improve your hitting or your defense.

When you're playing pepper you push the bat towards the ball. And you want to be level at contact. But I don't want to have the bat going that way. I want to lift *up* level on it. Those are things that I picked up. Nobody ever told me to do that.

Myself with John Wayne.

I met him twice. This time was at a Jimmy Fund event up in Boston. The little guy between us is Red Buttons. Bruce Cabot and Patrick Wayne—the Duke's son—that's them on the left.

John Wayne just absolutely was something special. Oh, Geez, yes. I thought he was always the best. I would sit in the back of the damn theater—1934, '35, and '36, and at a double header, double feature, I would go in there and I would be in the back. God, I couldn't wait for the damn thing to start. Here it started. It played about half of the first reel and I never will forget—this is as honest as I could ever say anything in my life—I'm watching that movie and I remember when I got up from my seat and stretched a little bit. I said, "I don't know whether this guy can act or not, but I sure like to watch him." I said that to my buddy. Even today I could be here and we would be talking, and if I heard his voice in the other room, even knowing it might just be on television, he would make me pause.

What a thrill, just an honest thrill, it was to meet Erroll Garner back in the late 1950s. Oh, he was a great, great pianist, wrote *Misty*, and, oh, how he could play. Swing was my favorite kind of music, but I loved jazz too, and Erroll was just brilliant, just so damn good at whatever he did, whatever he played.

Another spring training and another injury. In 1959 the Red Sox moved from Sarasota to Arizona. Tom Yawkey worked out a deal with Horace Stoneham to train at the Giants camp out there.

Before I left the Keys, though, I was loosened up, swinging a bat—and I felt something in my neck. I figured, hell, it would work itself out. But it didn't.

I was in no shape to play, although I *did* play when the team flew out to San Diego for a couple games. I didn't mind being home at all. I doubled in the second game out there, but *boy* it hurt. Once I felt good enough though to pitch a little batting practice. Was that ever a mistake.

The regular season started, and I was on the D.L. Didn't play an inning until May 12. Went 0 for 5. Then I proceeded to raise my average. All the way up to .045 after a week.

God, what a miserable, awful, *frustrating* year. If it wasn't my neck, it was a groin pull. I couldn't hit a lick. Didn't break the .200 barrier until late May. Late May! In September I finally started to hit a little and got my average up to .254. Still pretty damn poor.

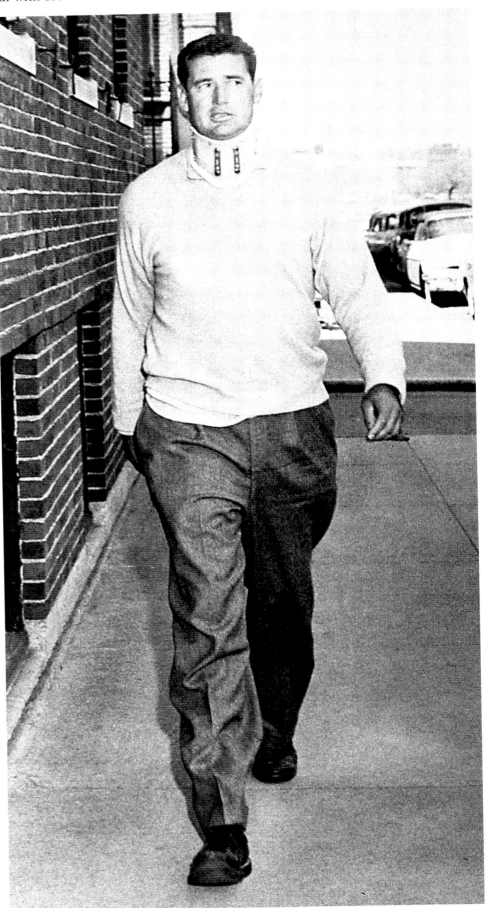

We trained in Arizona in 1960 and Ty Cobb came to visit. Cobb was a great

hitter, but we didn't always see eye-to-eye on hitting. He'd criticize me on drawing too many walks or on not hitting to left against that damned Williams Shift. He was a great hitter, but his style was totally different than mine.

But Cobb and Gene Tunney—the heavyweight champion—were the two class guys as far as being smart about their profession and smart about their actions after they *stopped* being athletes. Cobb was a millionaire. I was impressed.

On June 18, 1960 I hit my 500th homer, off a Cleveland righthander named Wynne Hawkins. I hit it over the left-field wall at Municipal Stadium.

That little sign reminds me of a friend of mine. A few times in the 1950s I'd get to thinking about quitting. I wasn't getting any younger and it wasn't getting any easier.

In the summer of 1954, I met a guy in the Baltimore train station. He said if I ended up playing a little while longer I could pass so-and-so in *this* category and so-and-so in *that* category. And this—and that—and the other thing. But the guy was right.

His name was Ed Mifflin. He was *100 percent* right. He was the first guy that said, "God, you don't want *him* to hit more home runs than *you*, do you? Do you want him to do *this*, and you not do *that*?" He talked a lot of sense to me, and I started to think about it. He kept me going. He was some kind of baseball nut. Hell of a nice guy.

Every time there are good hitters leaving the game, there are good hitters coming up. Here I am talking with Roger Maris, in July 1960, my last season. He was having a good season. Won the MVP award, beat out Mickey Mantle by three votes. It's a shame he's not in the Hall of Fame. Even though McGwire and Sosa have broken his record, his 61 homers was still a tremendous accomplishment. You know, Roger Maris' record—61—lasted longer than Ruth's 60. And Maris did it playing in the shadow of Mickey Mantle, putting even *more* pressure on him.

Not too many people know it, but when I up hung up my Red Sox uniform I had a chance to stay in the game in a Yankee uniform. The Yankees made me an offer. I could come down to New York, and all I had to do was pinch hit. That was it.

I wasn't interested. New York was too busy a place and I was going to quit because I knew I couldn't do it anymore. Geez, I was tired. I was on second base one day and I looked toward the mound and I saw the pitcher, I was at second base and I looked in and there was third base. I thought, Jeez, I had to run around this way to get to home. That's a long ways. I used to get sick every damn September. I was worn out. Worn out.

That last day, Joe Cronin came down on the field, down into the dugout, threw his arm around me. He was American League president now, and I was glad he was there for me. He had been my manager when I was a rookie, just breaking in, green as that Big Green Monster. Now he was there when it was all ending.

A lot of people later said they were at this game. Actually only 10,454 showed up.

72 | RAIN CHECK

IN THE EVENT OF POSTPONEMENT
THIS COUPON WILL ADMIT THE HOLDER
TO THE GAME NUMBERED HEREON.
NOT GOOD IF DETACHED FROM ORIGINAL
RAIN CHECK.

GRANDSTAND

Est.Pr. $1.91
Fed. Tax .09 **Total $2.00**

If legal game is not played or not resched-
uled with this same ticket valid, this rain
check may be exchanged at box office for
a ticket of the same price, if available, for
any future regularly scheduled American
League game of the current season.

NO MONEY REFUNDED

**BOSTON AMERICAN LEAGUE
BASEBALL COMPANY**

SEC.	ROW	SEAT
26	17	1

GAME		
72	SEPT. 1960 28	
	RAIN CHECK	

God, this was such a tough, gut-wrenching moment for me. I was so glad it was over, yes I was, but it hurt so much too. Sure, hitting was work—but it was such *bleepin' fun* too. God, I loved it.

Curt Gowdy—he was the Red Sox announcer then, a wonderful man, a great friend of mine—he introduced me and said some kind words. Then I spoke: "Despite some of the terrible things written about me—and they *were* terrible things, I'd like to forget them but can't—my stay in Boston has been the most wonderful part of my life. If someone should ask me the one place I'd want to play if I had to do all over again, I would say Boston, for it has the greatest owner in baseball and the greatest fans in America."

I'm told some of the knights of the keyboard didn't like those remarks, thought it was bush.

But I meant *every goddamn word* of what I said.

Steve Barber started that last game, and he developed into a good pitcher, but that day he was lousy, just wild all over the place. Didn't get anybody out in the first inning, and Jack Fisher came in to pitch for the Orioles. Fisher got me out twice on fly balls. The air was heavy, damp—and it was tough to get a ball out of the park. Then in the eighth I faced him again. I figured it would be my last time up, my last time in the game, my last time in Boston, my last time, period. Oh, how I wanted to hit one out, to go out on top, to do it right.

First pitch—ball one. Next pitch—right past me. Never got so much as a sliver on the ball. Boy, that steamed me, Teddy Ballgame didn't miss too many like that. Then Fisher comes in with another fastball. I swung, I connected, and it just kept going farther and farther into right center. Bam! Right into the bullpen. Oh, how that crowd cheered. Tip my cap? Yeah, I thought about it, but . . . nah, I couldn't do it, just didn't feel right. No, not then.

Throwing out the first pitch in Pittsburgh at the 1960 World Series.

I always loved fishing, wherever I was. In San Diego, in Minnesota, in New England, in Florida, Canada… wherever I was.

Of course, you can't fish that much *during* a baseball season—or at least not as much as you'd like. But once I retired, oh, that was a different story. Theodore Samuel Williams entered into a new phase of life— and the word went out: Fish beware. Mr. Williams is loose now and he has fishing on his mind.

Oh, those were wonderful, wonderful days.

Tying flies is an art, and I spent a lot of time trying to get it right.

President Bush once took me on a little tour, into the room next to the Lincoln Bedroom. Right there was a great collection of fishing flies. Beauties. If that didn't top off a visit to the White House, I don't know what would.

I wrote *Fishing the Big Three* with John Underwood in 1982. It's not as well known as *My Turn at Bat* or *The Science of Hitting*, but it's a damn good book.

The "Big Three" are tarpon—a real tackle-buster—bonefish, and Atlantic salmon. To me they're the triple crown of fishing. Each one is a challenge, each one a *great* game fish. I've caught *well* over a thousand of each so I ought to know.

The tarpon's been around a long time. It's prehistoric. You find them in the Atlantic, all the way from Brazil to North Carolina. I've fished for them in Texas. And I've fished for them in Costa Rica—at the mouth of the Parismina River. There are so many there, you could almost damn walk across them.

But Florida's just terrific for tarpon. Tarpon fishing was wonderful around my old home, at Islamorada on the Florida Keys. And actually, it was wonderful all the way to Key West. And the tarpon fishing is just about as good near where I live now in Hernando.

Hernando's not on the water, no, it's a little ways inland. But it's not far from Homosassa Springs on the Gulf of Mexico. That's where there's great tarpon fishing, and the tarpon are just a bit larger there too.

Bonefish. Well, bonefish is why I moved to the Keys in the first place. I had been working my way down the peninsula actually. It was snook that brought me down to the Everglades. That was about 1943, when I was in the service and stationed at Pensacola. A great fisherman, an outstanding guy, named Lee Cuddy tipped

NOW IN PAPERBACK
TED WILLIAMS' CLASSIC GUIDE TO THE "SCIENCE OF FISHING"

FISHING "THE BIG THREE"
Tarpon, Bonefish, Atlantic Salmon

Ted Williams and John Underwood

me off about bonefish in the Keys. The bonefish isn't a very big fish, but it's a *game* fish. A fighter. Pound-for-pound the *toughest* fish you'd ever want to catch. I first went to the Keys in 1947, and I caught 67 bonefish. Not too long after, I got myself a house in the Keys. Not much of a house. But I didn't need much.

When you ask me about Atlantic salmon, you have to ask me about the Miramichi River in New Brunswick. Oh, what a wonderful place. The beauty of it, the serenity. You know, I didn't really fully appreciate it at first. I went up to shoot a TV show. It was cold. It was crowded, a line of guys casting left and right. Guys casting in front of you. But pretty soon I realized how good it would be if I had a pool of my own, tied my own flies. After that I'd fly right up after the end of each baseball season to catch Atlantic salmon, which I consider the greatest fish there is.

TED WILLIAMS

At a testimonial in January 1966—the night before I was elected to the Hall of Fame. That's Carl Yastrzemski on the right—a great player. He had an intensity that I probably never had as much, even though *I* was certainly intense. But he … Wow!

When I saw him take batting practice the first time, I said to the guys down there, "When he starts cocking the bat he looks like he's wrapping himself up like a spring. Boy, he's really ready to do it."

You know what Bobby Doerr once said about Yastrzemski? He said Yaz had the single best season he ever saw. That was that Triple Crown year he had in 1967. Best season he ever saw—and Doerr played with *me* for a full decade!

THAT'S ME AND THE OLD PERFESSER, CASEY STENGEL.
WE WERE GOING INTO THE HALL OF FAME TOGETHER
THAT YEAR. IF YOU HAD TOLD ME THEN THAT I'D BE FOL-
LOWING IN CASEY'S FOOTSTEPS—MANAGING—IN A FEW
YEARS, I'D HAVE TOLD YOU YOU WERE NUTS.

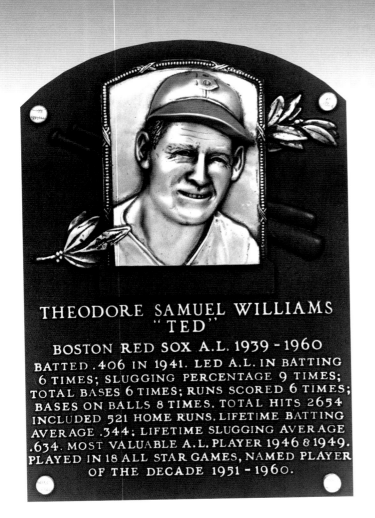

THEODORE SAMUEL WILLIAMS
"TED"
BOSTON RED SOX A.L. 1939-1960
BATTED .406 IN 1941. LED A.L. IN BATTING
6 TIMES; SLUGGING PERCENTAGE 9 TIMES;
TOTAL BASES 6 TIMES; RUNS SCORED 6 TIMES;
BASES ON BALLS 8 TIMES. TOTAL HITS 2654
INCLUDED 521 HOME RUNS. LIFETIME BATTING
AVERAGE .344; LIFETIME SLUGGING AVERAGE
.634. MOST VALUABLE A.L. PLAYER 1946 & 1949.
PLAYED IN 18 ALL STAR GAMES, NAMED PLAYER
OF THE DECADE 1951-1960.

My Hall of Fame plaque at Cooperstown.

I can't say it was a surprise I was elected. No, I did deserve it, and there was no way the writers could ignore my numbers—what I had accomplished, what I had *worked* to accomplish. But there was the question back then if you'd go in first ballot on not. DiMaggio took *three* ballots. *DiMaggio*! Hank Greenberg, Jimmie Foxx—*not* first ballot! So even though I wasn't really *surprised*, I've got to say I was still *moved*. How can you *not* be moved?

In 1966 they—the sportswriters—voted me into the Hall of Fame. Voted me and Casey Stengel in together. I knew I could never outtalk Casey. But in my hotel room in Cooperstown I wrote out an acceptance speech of my own. Here's how it went:

I guess every player thinks about going into the Hall of Fame. Now that the moment has come for me, I find it difficult to say what is really in my heart, but I know it is the greatest thrill of my life. I received two-hundred-and-eighty odd votes from the writers. I know I didn't have two-hundred-and-eighty odd friends among the writers. I know they voted for me because they felt in their minds and in their hearts that I rated it. And I want to say to them thank you from the bottom of my heart.

"Today I am thinking about a lot of things. I am thinking about my playground director in San Diego, Rodney Luscomb, my high school coach, Wos Caldwell, and my managers, who had so much patience with me—fellows like Frank Shellenback, Donie Bush, Joe Cronin, and Joe McCarthy. I am thinking of Eddie Collins who had so much faith in me; to be in the Hall with him particularly, as well as those other great players, is a great honor. I'm sorry Eddie isn't here today.

"I'm thinking of Tom Yawkey. I have always said it: Tom Yawkey is the greatest owner in baseball. I was lucky to have played on the club he owned and I'm grateful to him for being here today. But I'd not be leveling if I left it at that. Ballplayers are not born great. They're not born great hitters or pitchers or managers. And luck isn't a big factor. No one has come up with a substitute for hard work. I've never met a great player who didn't have to work harder at learning to play ball than anything else he ever did. To me it was the greatest fun I ever had which probably explains why today I feel both humility and pride, because God let me play the game and learn to be good at it.

"The other day Willie Mays hit his 522nd home run. He has gone past me, and he's pushing, and I say to him, go get 'em Willie. Baseball gives every American boy the chance to excel, not just to be as good as anybody else, but to be better. This is the nature of man and the name of the game. I hope some day Satchel Paige and Josh Gibson will be voted into the Hall of Fame as symbols of the great Negro League players who are not here only because they weren't given the chance.

"As time goes on I'll be thinking baseball, teaching baseball, and arguing baseball, to keep it right on top of American sports, just as it is in Japan, Mexico, Venezuela, and other Latin American and South American countries. I know Casey feels the same way. I also know I'll lose a dear friend if I don't stop talking. I'm eating into his time, and that is unforgivable. So in closing, I am grateful and know how lucky I am to have been born an American and to have had the chance to play the game I love, the greatest game."

After I retired as a player I opened up a baseball camp for kids in Lakeville, Massachusetts. I've got to admit it was fun hanging around and helping kids learn the game.

I went to camp as a kid, a YMCA camp. Art Linkletter was one of the counselors, although that didn't mean anything at the time. Wasn't much to it, at the bottom of a gully. Somebody stole the money my mother sent me off with. One of my *big* activities was peeling potatoes. Boy, I hated that.

Lakeville was a *lot* better.

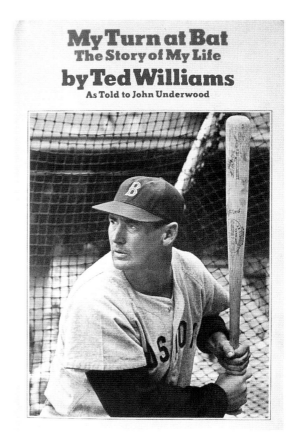

In June 1969 I published my memoirs:

My Turn At Bat: The Story of My Life. I had a great collaborator in John Underwood, a wonderful Miami writer. He's a great guy, an honest, good man.

The *New York Times* called the book "The portrait of an original who is unrepentant about being better than anybody else." Well, what's *wrong* with being better? What's wrong with being the *best*? If you go out not trying to be the best, well … I don't know what the point is.

The initial part of a baseball swing is not truly a swing. Now, push out, push out. You got power all the way there don't you? Push out. Keep pushing. Now you can start turning your hips. Now you got power all the way through that swing now.

Originally the power comes from the fact that you had to get the bat out front. Now, this is the quickest way to get the bat in front right there. Then you can do a lot of stuff from there. Or you start to hit it and it's up, you bring your hands and swing up.

Swinging up is always important. Try this demonstration. Pretend you're swinging down at an imaginary ball. Have someone resist you. Have them block your motion. Now swing *up* with the ball and keep going. Same thing with having someone resist you. See, you're *a lot* stronger swinging up, aren't you?

My famous chart. Most people know it from my book *The Science of Hitting*, but it actually first appeared in an article in *Sports Illustrated*. I got the idea from Paul Waner. He had something like it. We doctored it up and colored it up. The more I saw it, the more I liked it.

The idea is pretty simple: get your pitch—and when it arrives swing at it. Certain areas, certain choices, *make* you a .400 hitter, a .350 hitter. Other areas, it's the pitcher's game. So when you have a choice—on that first pitch, or when you're ahead 1-and-0, 2-and-0, 3-and-0, *lay off* the pitches you can't hit *well*, where the odds aren't in your favor.

Back in the '50s there had been some talk about me managing the Red Sox. That was after they fired Lou Boudreau. Mr. Yawkey and Joe Cronin said they'd get me whatever help I needed.

I wasn't interested. It was a bad team, and I'd just end up fired like the manager of every other bad team. Right after I quit playing there was even a rumor I'd be a coach with the Chicago Cubs. Phil Wrigley had a "College of

Coaches" then that alternated as manager. So it was pretty much a managing job. That rumor wasn't even true.

So I had never really had much interest at all in managing. Then along came Bob Short. He bought the Washington Senators in 1969. They were an expansion team, formed back in '61—never were any good. They even finished *10th* a couple of times. But Short called me one day down in the Keys, asked if I wanted to replace Jim Lemon as manager. I said "no." He called again—same answer. He got Joe Cronin to work on me. And he *really* impressed me with how smart he was. Just about the smartest guy I ever met. I never could understand why he was a *Democrat*.

Anyway, he wore me down. I must admit money had something to do with it. He offered me $1.5 million—and back then that was *real* money. I even had an option to buy 10 percent of the club.

President Nixon threw out the first pitch of the 1969 season. That's Commissioner Bowie Kuhn standing next to me.

I wasn't the only new kid in town. Vince Lombardi had just taken over the Washington Redskins and District of Columbia Mayor Walter Washington presented both of us with the keys to the city.

The umpires always explain the ground rules to both managers before they start a ballgame. Happened to me here—my first game managing at Fenway. The last thing I had on my mind then was the damn ground rules. Boy, that was an exciting moment. And you know what? We won that day. Nine-to-three. Made it all just right, I'll tell you, just perfect.

Coaching Mike Epstein.

One of the best parts of managing—and once you *do* manage you realize there isn't a *wide range* of best parts—is to work on your players' hitting. It was tremendously satisfying.

The year before I took over the Senators, they hit a whopping .224. They drew 454 walks. They hit 124 homers. Needless, to say, they finished dead last.

I got the team average up to .251. They walked 630 times—more selective. Homered 148 times.

Took Eddie Brinkman from .187 to .266. Told him to quit trying to hit the ball in the air. With his body he could never hit it far enough. Told him to get around quicker too. When you're swinging late you have a tendency to pop the ball up—and that was *poison* for a hitter like Brinkman.

Got Frank Howard to cut down on his strikeouts, from 141 to 96. Got him to increase his walks. Hell, he was so strong, all he had to do was *look at the ball* and it would go out. Go out from pure *fear*. Hell, he didn't need to try and kill it.

You know it's a funny thing. A guy like Howard has to be a smarter hitter than a guy like Brinkman. What do

I mean by that? Well, a pitcher doesn't have to be too afraid of making a mistake to Brinkman. Make a mistake to him—it's a single. Make a mistake to Howard—it's across the Potomac. Walk Brinkman—it's the same as if you've given up a single. Walk Howard—and you've saved three bases. Maybe *saved your life.*

What's all that mean? It means that Brinkman will actually get *better* pitches to hit. The pitchers will be a lot more careful to Howard. Pitch more *around* the plate, *off* the plate. So he has to be more *selective.* *Think* more at bat.

There's a chart in my book, *The Science of Hitting*—check it out—it shows the overall improvement in Washington. Brinkman. Howard. Epstein, McMullen. Unser. Bernie Allen. Hank Allen. All better hitters. And that translates into a winning record.

TED WILLIAMS

Father's Day in Washington in 1970. My son John-Henry had been born in 1968. I was so

happy when he was born. I gave him the name John-Henry because I thought a name like that conveyed strength. He

hasn't disappointed me. He's been my strong right arm the last few years.

A year later—in 1971—he got a little sister, Claudia.

After my first season in Washington, I took off for Africa, to Zambia. John Underwood went along and we hunted along the Kufue River and on the Zambesi. I bagged some kudo, a warthog, a reedbuck.

I remember hunting Cape buffalo. We had to crawl on our bellies to hunt them, for about 150 yards. Oh, that was rough, dragging along the ground, carrying that .458. We got to about a hundred yards from the herd—then one of them charged. Charged! I got off a shot and it ripped through his shoulder. Then I got off another one—into the septum. The third shot I put right through his brain—right under the horns.

I killed several animals in Africa. But I never did like hunting that well, that kind of hunting, because I never did learn how to shoot where I *should* have been shooting at those animals. I always shot too high. In other words, I would shoot in the middle of his shoulder, but should have shot a foot lower. On a fatal shot you want to get it down in that area, it has more effect on the animal.

Funny thing about that trip. I was in Nairobi. And an Episcopal missionary came up to me—I was in a five-and-dime store there—and asked if Frank Howard was still overswinging. I assured him I was working on it.

It was on that trip that I got the news about being named American League Manager of the Year. Bob Addie called me. I couldn't believe it.

MANAGER OF THE YEAR

TED WILLIAMS, LAST OF THE .400 HITTERS WHILE PLAYING WITH BOSTON, HAS BEEN SELECTED THE ASSOCIATED PRESS' AMERICAN LEAGUE MANAGER OF THE YEAR, IN HIS ROOKIE YEAR LEADING THE WASHINGTON SENATORS. THE SELECTION CAME ON THE BASIS OF A NATIONWIDE VOTE BY SPORTS WRITERS AND BROADCASTERS. WILLIAMS MANAGED THE SENATORS IN THEIR FIRST WINNING SEASON IN 17 YEARS.

Managing is not for the faint of heart—or for those unwilling to express themselves. Here, Don Mincher, my first baseman, and I are *expressing* ourselves to umpire Jim Odom. This is actually an unusual picture. I don't think you can find too many of me jawing with umpires. I didn't much. They were fair to me—some of my "admirers" might have said *too* fair with me, but they *were* fair with me. And I had respect for them. They had a job to do—and they pretty much did it decently.

In my first year as manager the team hustled, *really* hustled. They hit. I got them up to fourth—they had never been higher than sixth before.

I won Manager of the Year. Beat out Earl Weaver and Billy Martin. Hell, I thought, this wasn't so hard after all.

Then reality set in. We fell to fifth—last—in 1970. But we had some talent—Howard, Epstein, Brinkman, Aurelio Rodriguez—a damn good third baseman we stole from the Angels—Dick Bosman, Joe Coleman. We could have rebounded. But in the offseason we traded away Rodriguez, Brinkman, and Coleman to Detroit for Denny McLain. Boy, was I mad. That trade gutted our infield and gave away one of our best pitchers. On the other hand, I *wanted* Short to trade Mike Epstein. Thought he was at peak value. Short wouldn't. We sunk even further. Never had a chance.

In 1972 Bob Short moved the team to Texas, to Arlington. Thought that would increase attendance. Well, the people in Texas weren't any more interested in seeing a bad team than the people in Washington were. We lost 100 games and finished last.

I had another year on my contract, but that was it. I had managed my last game. How crappy was that last team I had? Well, the next year Texas went through three managers, and two of them were named Whitey Herzog and Billy Martin. They lost *105* games.

I always kept my eye on what the Red Sox were up to, and it felt good to see them finally get back on track in the 1970s when guys like Darrell Johnson and Don Zimmer were managing. Here's Zim along with my old friend Joe Cronin.

WITH YAZ AT WINTER HAVEN IN 1983.

Bobby Doerr and I go all the way back to when we played together as kids on the San Diego Padres.

He was a great hitter, fine power for a second baseman. A tremendous fielder too. People forget that. I don't know why it took so long for him to get into the Hall of Fame.

No one had worn #9 for the Sox since I retired in 1960,

and, in fact, there was an announcement at the time that no one ever *would*. But they didn't make that big a deal out of such things back then. So in 1984 the team got around to holding an actual ceremony to make it all official. The nice thing about the event was they also retired Joe Cronin's #4.

In July 1985 they unveiled a statue at the Baseball Hall of Fame by Armand LaMontagne. Jean Yawkey commissioned it, and it was a fantastic honor. I was there for the unveiling along with my special friend Louise Kaufman. I've got to admit I cried when they unveiled it.

Armand LaMontagne is a true artist—

and in two mediums, sculpture and painting. He's done a number of wonderful renditions of Teddy Ballgame. That great wood sculpture of me in Cooperstown is his and so is the statue in my museum, of me fishing. I really like this portrait of me based on a photo taken early in my career.

ARMAND LaMONTAGNE

Was it a better game back then? That's a *damn* good question.

And, over the years I've had different answers—and I think I've been right each time.

First off, let me just state unequivocally that I *felt* that the time after World War II was a tremendous, wonderful, time for baseball. I'm so glad I had the opportunity to play back then. DiMaggio. Feller. Musial. Kiner. Spahn. Pesky. Doerr. Slaughter. Boudreau. Rizzuto. Fantastic players. Good young players like Dick Wakefield. Alvin Dark.

You had *so* many talented players coming back from the service—hundreds of them. And they were *hungry*. They *wanted* to play. And they had spent a lot of time as kids playing ball all the time. That's important. Nothing can take the place of being out there, taking your swings, anticipating situations. Learning everything you could about the game.

I think that deteriorated in time. By the '60s and '70s baseball wasn't as good. It just wasn't. The players weren't as skilled in the fundamentals. Expansion had watered things down. The minors were withering on the vine. And the parks! All big concrete ashtrays! Too big for decent hitting. Damn pitchers' paradises like Dodger Stadium and the Astrodome. Thank God the pendulum has swung back the other way.

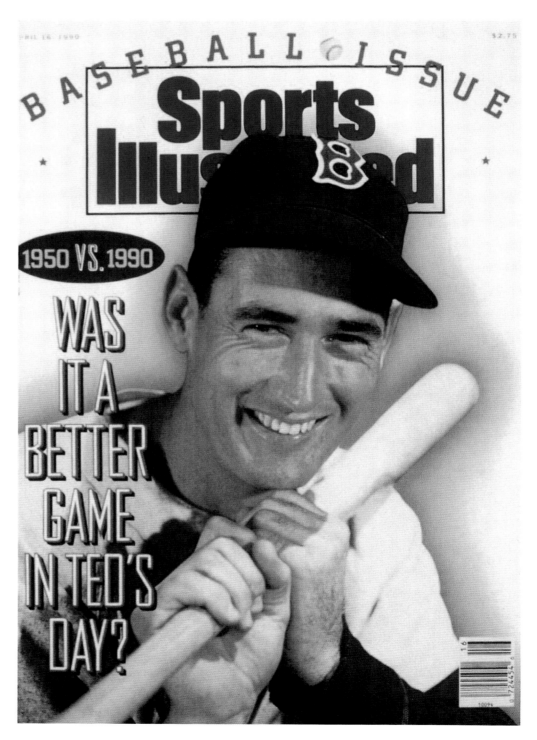

Ihad Moxie. Yogi had Yoo-Hoo (and Ty Cobb had Coca-Cola—he was *really* smart), but Berra and I both got together for some commercials for J. J. Nissen—that's a regional New England bakery. Actually I had done some commercials for them before, with my friend Bud Leavitt. Bud's a sportswriter from up in Maine, and we've known each other damn near forever. We first met back in my rookie year back in '39. We've hunted and fished together all over the place. We did another commercial up on the Miramichi in New Brunswick.

People ask me if I really drank Moxie.

I sure did, and I kind of liked Moxie. That might have been my best chance that I ever had of possibly making some money, I mean *real* money. The reason was I got in on a stock deal with them. I had an option to buy so much Moxie at a certain price. Moxie at that time needed a lot of help and was a little bit on the brink. The guy that we were working with didn't have an idea in hell of what a good drink should taste like. We signed the contract, we got this, we got that. We got three or four bottling people up there and changed the flavor a little bit.

Then they came up with a root beer. Nine million companies did root beer—Hires Root Beer and A&W and all the other root beers out there—that were good. No imagination, see. So it didn't go over very big, nor did we make as much money as we should have. We figured if the thing really went and with a hell of a drink, you could improve that drink enough to get it going with the publicity they had going around with me—and Moxie was a very popular drink. But I think you can improve it, even now. Anyway, see, you make booboos. I didn't know anything about soft drinks or anything else, or how to make money.

Ted Williams says *Make Mine* **MOXIE**

T E D   W I L L I A M S

At the 1991 All-Star Game at Toronto's SkyDome. It was the 50th anniversary

of .406 and the 56-game streak—and Joe DiMaggio and I made the rounds together.

Jean Yawkey invited me up to Boston in 1991 for "Ted Williams Day." I didn't want to do it, but it was always tough turning her down. Mayor Flynn proclaimed it was "Ted Williams Day" in the whole damn city and even announced he was renaming a part of Lansdowne Street—that part just in back of left field—"Ted Williams Way." A lot of my old teammates were there. Bobby Doerr. Johnny Pesky. Dom DiMaggio. Jimmy Piersall. Carl Yastrzemski.

They had a ceremony at home plate—they *always* have a ceremony at home plate—and I thought I'd give the fans a little surprise. I hid a Red Sox cap in my pocket and reached in and tipped it to the fans. I did it, as I said:

"So they can never write, ever again that I was hard-headed, so they can never write again that I never tipped my hat to the crowd, today I tip my hat. I tip my hat to all the people in New England, the greatest sports fans on earth."

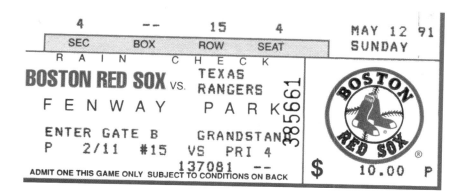

John-Henry in his office in Hernando, just down the road from my

museum. A lot of folks know that John-Henry has been handling my business affairs for the past few years, Ted Williams Family Enterprises. He's done a damn good job too. Watches out for me. What many people may not know is that he also has a business of his own, hitter.net. An internet company. Doing very well in that as well. Knows his stuff. Knows high tech. Knows the *future* of business. I'm proud of him.

Home on the range about 1988. That's Slugger, my Dalmatian, my friend. He's gone now. We tried our damnedest to keep him around, gave him the best food, tried everything. But it was finally his time. It hurts like hell to think of him. God, I miss that little fellow.

When they first came to me with the idea of a Ted Williams Museum, I was not *impressed.* Hell, museums are for guys like Winston Churchill, MacArthur, Nixon, Cardinal Cushing, John Glenn—hell!—even John Wayne. Not me.

But they worked on me, and I thought, well, it might be worthwhile for youngsters. You know, to encourage excellence, to help give something back to baseball. Sam Tamposi donated the land, Gerry Nash pitched in, and the idea took off. The design is

interesting, different. We couldn't quite figure out how to organize the place. Then somebody got the idea: a diamond. So the Museum displays are organized like a diamond—four sides—and that's how fans, visitors, look around the place. We've added a couple of wings since the original idea. There's the Hitter's Hall of Fame on one end. And on the opposite end, there's a little auditorium, complete with bleachers. Oh yeah, if you look around you'll see the ceiling and the trim and stuff is painted a familiar shade of green. It's goddamn *Big Green Monster Fenway green.* Same paint, same brand, same shade, used to paint Fenway.

We opened the doors on February 9, 1994. It was quite the event. We had 37 Hall of Famers there. Joe DiMaggio. Stan Musial. Monte Irvin. My buddy Bobby Doerr. My daughter Bobby Jo. My son John-Henry. A great time.

In 1995 we opened that wing I was telling you about, The Hitters Hall of Fame. George Bush—the father—and Barbara Bush were there. Musial. Mantle. Mays. Enos Slaughter. Frank Robinson. A lot of great hitters showed up.

And people *keep* showing up, thank the Lord. Since then we've had some great inductees, some great honorees. Killebrew. Aparicio. McCovey. Eddie Mathews. Reggie Jackson. McGwire. Sheffield. Piazza. Yount. Brett. Boggs. Great young kids like Nomar Garciaparra and Scott Rolen. And some great friends, wonderful friends, like Curt Gowdy, Tommy Lasorda, Bob Costas.

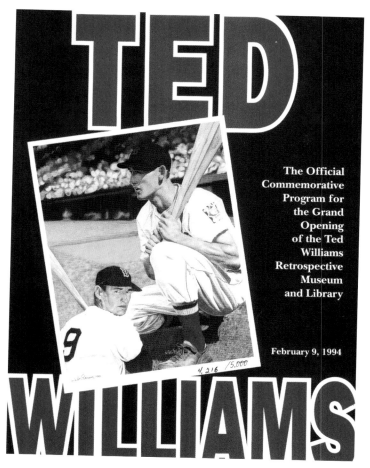

The Official
Commemorative
Program for
the Grand
Opening
of the Ted
Williams
Retrospective
Museum
and Library

February 9, 1994

February 9, 1995
$15.00

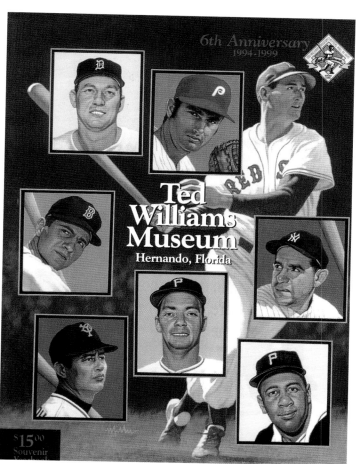

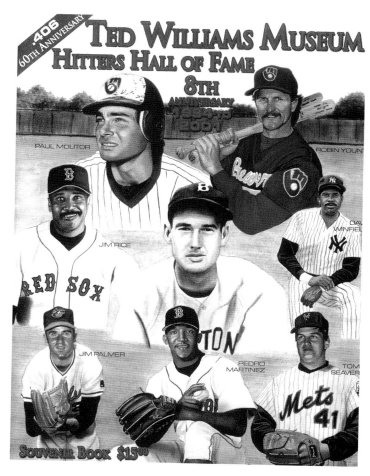

WE INDUCTED REGGIE JACKSON INTO OUR HITTERS
HALL OF FAME IN 1998. A GREAT POWER HITTER, A
WONDERFUL CLUTCH HITTER. A LOT OF STRIKEOUTS—
TOO MANY—BUT WHEN HE HIT 'EM HE MADE 'EM COUNT.

Myself and Johnny Pesky at a Red Sox Hall of Fame dinner in 1995.

I haven't said much about Johnny yet in this book. So I better now. Pesky was not only a fine ballplayer, but a fine all-around athlete. Box. Wrestle. Hoops. You name it, he could do just anything but swim. Sink like a rock.

He and I went into the service together in '42. Trained together at Amherst, Massachusetts. He wasn't much of a pilot, even though he denies it, but he made officer before I did.

He got a bad rap on that play in the '46 Series. Nobody gave him a heads-up, and Enos Slaughter just ran like hell to reach home.

You know, I've had some tremendous honors, some absolutely tremendous honors for a skinny kid from San Diego. But one of the absolutely nicest, most meaningful was having that tunnel, the Ted Williams Tunnel, the "Big Dig," named after me.

It becomes a bigger thrill all the time. It becomes a bigger spectacle for me every time. That thing has got so much background to it and so much engineering way ahead of its time. And the saddest part of it all is the guy that was responsible for it, a great guy, Governor Bill Weld, he didn't get confirmed for God's sakes, for ambassador to Mexico. He'd have been great for that job.

WITH RED SOX MANAGER JIMY WILLIAMS
IN CLEARWATER IN MARCH 1998.

THE THING ABOUT FISHING IS IT'S
THE WHOLE GODDAMN PACKAGE.
IT'S NOT JUST THE CASTING, THE
ANTICIPATION. IT'S THE BEAUTY,
THE PEACE OF WHERE YOU ARE.
GOSH, IT'S WONDERFUL, JUST SO
DAMNED WONDERFUL.

The last time I went out bass fishing.

TED WILLIAMS

This is the logo of the Ted Williams League. Maybe you've never heard of it. It's still young, still pretty small, but it's growing and it's a good idea, a smart idea.

First off, it's not just another version of Little League or Connie Mack or Babe Ruth with my name slapped on to it. If they did that, well, I'd be honored, but otherwise there wouldn't be all that much point to it.

No, the Ted Williams League is *different*. Baseball's a difficult game. *Hitting* a baseball is the toughest thing to do in sports. I think you've heard me make that point a few times over the years.

Well, the rest of baseball isn't that easy either. And it doesn't get any easier if you're some pint-sized little kid who has trouble gripping the bat or throwing the ball over the plate or even throwing out the runner at first on a grounder.

It's *hard* for little kids. And when little kids aren't *having fun*, when they don't feel they're *accomplishing something*, they don't *do it*.

That's why myself and a fellow named Steve Ferroli established this league in 1997. Here's the idea. We change the dimensions to make the game fit the kids. A slightly smaller ball—easier to grip, both for pitchers and fielders. Thinner bat—same thing. Longer bat—the kid can cover more of the plate. A smaller plate, just 14 inches across—to encourage the pitcher to s-l-o-w d-o-w-n and get it over the plate. Longer baselines—to make it easier to get the runners out on grounders.

Look, here's how it comes together. Everybody says a kid can't throw to 14 inches. They're wrong! What happens is the pitcher slows down a bit because he knows it's a smaller zone, and that's where this whole thing shines, because the little hitter starts thinking about hitting rather than being scared to death. Before you know it, the bats are swinging and now the hitter is getting himself out. I mean, here comes the ball traveling a bit slower but three inches outside and the little hitter swings and grounds out.

Well, if you know baseball, there are several lessons in that experience. So the kid learns how to hit—and not be afraid. And he learns restraint.

In 1999—when I was up in Boston for the All-Star Game—I got together with Einer Gustafson. He was the original "Jimmy" in the "Jimmy Fund." There's been a lot of Jimmys since. I wish none of them ever *had* to be Jimmys, dammit, but I'm glad we've done what we could to help. Geez, I wish we could have done *more*.

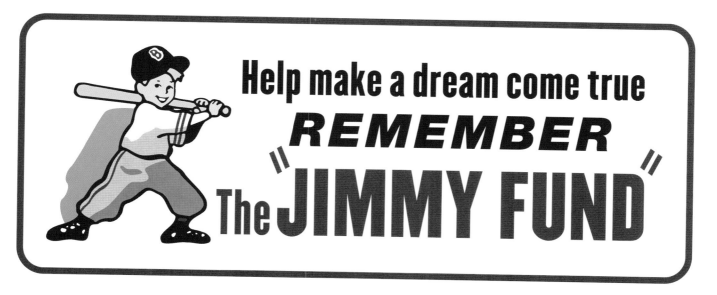

I want Baseball to right an injustice.

It's not to me. It's to the memory of one of the greatest hitters, greatest players, who ever played this game. I'm talking about Shoeless Joe Jackson. And it's about time we say he's paid the price, served his sentence—served his sentence for a crime no court of law ever found him guilty of.

Right now, the Baseball Hall of Fame has most—I say most—of the greatest players who ever lived. But when you look at all the measurements of greatness, all the statistics, you can't help but notice that one of the very, very, very best isn't in Cooperstown.

And that's wrong. Damn wrong. And Baseball shouldn't tolerate injustice. It's too good for that.

Back in 1966 when I was fortunate enough to stand at the podium at the Hall of Fame and give my induction speech, I made a pitch for Satchel Paige's induction. It was wrong that he wasn't in the Hall of Fame, and it was just as big a wrong that his fellow Negro League greats were ignored.

We've undone part of that unfairness—although some qualified Negro Leaguers still remain out of Cooperstown. I know that Buck O'Neil and Monte Irvin will continue to counsel the Veterans Committee on that.

As to Joe Jackson's nomination and qualifications … I think I know a little about hitting. And Joe Jackson was one of the finest hitters of all time. Look at the numbers: a .356 lifetime average, third best ever. He hit .408 in his first full year in the majors. And he hit with power. Cobb spread his hands apart and punched out those hits. Jackson lashed away and pushed out a ton of doubles and triples, the real power hits of his day.

I'm not going to bore you with numbers. You can look them up as well as I can, maybe better. But I can tell you that anyone I talked to who saw Jackson play was just amazed at what he could do. Eddie Collins—a great guy, a great friend—was with Jackson on the White Sox. Collins told me, "Ted, you're the closest thing I ever saw to Joe Jackson. All I could think about when I saw Ted Williams was Joe Jackson."

When Babe Ruth wanted to model his swing after the perfect swing, it was Jackson he imitated—Jackson, with his big Black Betsy, whaling the tar out of the ball. Hitting for the third highest average in history. Hitting with power, triples all over the place.

The greatest natural hitter of all time is what some say. I think they may be right. And he could field too. His arm may have been better than Clemente's. When he started out in the semi-pros he was a pitcher, you know. Or at least he was until he broke his catcher's arm with a pitch.

Well, yes, you'll concede all that. You have to. Hell, how could anyone argue against Joe Jackson as a great hitter, great player. You can't. Don't even try.

Of course, there is that matter of the World Series. Let me tell you about Jackson and the Black Sox. I know all about them.

Now, Joe shouldn't have accepted money from a teammate, and he realized his error. He tried to give the money back. He tried to tell Comiskey, the White Sox owner, about the fix. But they wouldn't listen. Comiskey covered it up as much as Jackson did—maybe more. And there's Charles Albert Comiskey down the aisle from me in Cooperstown—and Shoeless Joe still waits outside.

How dishonest could Jackson have been in that 1919 Series? How much a fixer? He hit .375, slugged .563, got 12 hits—that was a record—and even homered, homered into the right-field bleachers in Cincinnati. Homers didn't come easy then. It was a dead ball. Hell, it was the only homer of the Series—by either team. And to top it off he led the Sox in RBIs and runs scored.

The White Sox made 12 errors in that Series. So did the Reds. How many did Jackson make? Zero. Of course, no jury ever convicted Jackson. Consider that. He was acquitted, walked out of the courthouse a free man. That is, until Judge Landis threw him out of baseball, threw him out for life. They say Landis was a vindictive man—but Joe served his sentence and paid his debt to baseball. Baseball can't impose a sentence longer than Judge Landis did. Joe Jackson's not alive anymore. He's served his sentence. It's time for Baseball to acknowledge his debt is paid; and for the Hall of Fame Committee on Veterans to list him as a nominee.

To move things along, I have requested that Joe Jackson's name be placed on the Hall of Fame ballot and have even given the Hall a legal memorandum in support of that request. Cooperstown should now act. It's time, and it's the right thing to do.

When I was younger, the Red Sox used to stop sometimes in Greenville, South Carolina—that's Jackson's home. And he was still alive. Oh, how I wish I had known that and could have stopped in to talk hitting with that man. It's too late, but it's not too late for him to come and join me—and all the other Hall of Famers—in Cooperstown. Come on in, Joe I'd say, your wait is over. Let's talk hitting.

My good friend Tricia Miranti.
We met in March 1994 when I started doing rehab—I had my second stroke that February. She was 17 then and had been confined to a wheelchair since she was 5—she had a brain aneurysm. Boy, what a lousy deal. We've made some progress together, shared some laughs, had some good times. I'm glad I've had the chance to get to know her. A terrific person. A fighter.

She's in college now. I'm proud of that, proud of her.

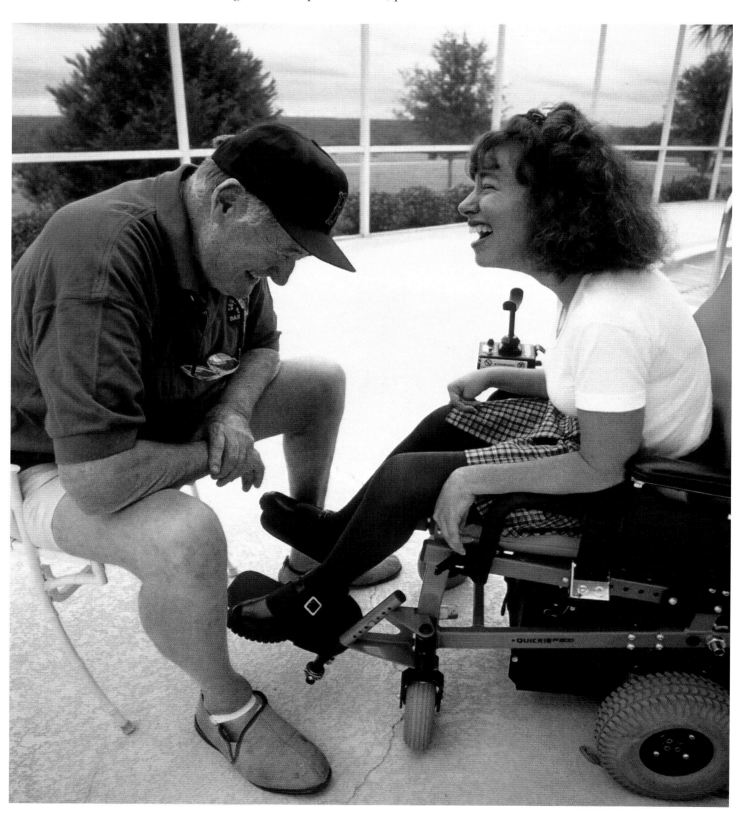

In June 2000 John-Henry and I helped launch a new version of monopoly, "Boston Red Sox Monopoly." It's neat, real neat. The tokens are made of pewter. The dice are in the Sox team colors, and you amass your Red Sox empire with luxury boxes and stadiums instead of hotels and houses. By the way, the "Ted Williams" card is only $50 less than the "Fenway Park" card.

Number 9 Meets Number 3—Dale Earnhardt. In the last few

years I've gotten interested in NASCAR. Yes, I have. Back in July 1999 they even made me grand
marshal for the Jiffy Lube 300 up in Loudon, New Hampshire. Helluva honor.

I watch a *lot* of NASCAR on TV. But when you see it in person, see all those cars flying around
the track, hear that noise, see the precision of their moves, wow, that's really something. That
really hooks you.

Tommy Lasorda's pretty smart for a pitcher.

He's one of the finest ambassadors baseball's ever had, a diamond in the rough, always talking up the game, making us all proud to have been a part of it. That's why I asked Tommy to be the master of ceremonies at my Hitters Hall of Fame festivities. In fact, I did more than *ask*—I told him he was going to do it—and he was going to do it *for five years*. Management always likes to lock talent into a long-term contract.

Here we are in Dodgertown in March 2000 for the opening of the Dodgers spring training season.

TED WILLIAMS

I confess. I've always been a Republican. Always will be too, I guess.

I supported Nixon in 1960. He was the greatest man I met—and a hell of a baseball fan. God, I damn near cry when I think about how he got involved with some of these things that helped destroy him. He didn't have the help around him he should have had. But when Mr. Kissinger, 30 years later, says he was a great man, well, he was a great man.

You might think a lot of politicians would have come down to the ballpark in Washington when I was managing the Senators, but they really didn't. This time though, we got a visit from Speaker of the House John McCormack—from Boston—and House

Minority Leader Gerry Ford. I really admired Ford. I think he was a hell of a man.

Oh yeah, one time Bob Short—he was from Minnesota—he set up a dinner for us with Eugene McCarthy. The next spring McCarthy—he used to play a little ball when he was younger—showed up at our spring training camp in a Senators uniform and went down on the field. I had to get him thrown off before he got himself killed.

In July 1991 President George Bush presented Joe DiMaggio and me with a Presidential Citation for our "contributions to baseball and good sportsmanship."

A few months later—in November 1991—President Bush gave me the Presidential Medal of Freedom, our nation's highest civilian honor. I was in some pretty good company. William F. Buckley, Jr. Betty Ford. Tip O'Neill. Russell Train, chairman of the World Wildlife and Conservation Fund. My plaque read:

THEODORE SAMUEL WILLIAMS
Awarded by
President George Bush
November 18, 1991
Theodore Samuel Williams—
Ted Williams, the "Splendid Splinter"—
is perhaps the greatest hitter of all time.
Williams made it look easy. He won six
batting titles, blasted 521 home runs,
and half a century ago amazed America
by becoming the last man to bat
over .400. He also gallantly served his
country in two wars and retired from
baseball as only a hero could—with a
home run in his final at bat. A conserva-
tionist, avid fisherman, and baseball Hall
of Famer, Ted Williams is a living legend.

In January 2000 I endorsed George W. Bush for President. Good man—like his father. And a survivor of the Texas Rangers— like me.

TED WILLIAMS

Just a couple of old Marine pilots getting together. In October 1998 John Glenn was about to go into space aboard the STS-95. Seventy-seven years old—and back into space. Not bad at all. I wish I could have gone up with him. That would have been something. But it was good to say hello to him, swap a few stories, and wish him well. He didn't let anybody down. Then again, he never did. Certainly not me.

I ran into Steven Tyler—the Aerosmith Steven Tyler—when they were launching John Glenn into space. Boy, they had everybody up there—President Clinton, governors, senators, rock stars. And some old ballplayers too.

My 80th birthday. That's my daughter Claudia—my youngest—with me. She's something special—an activities director at a treatment center that's not too far away from me, not too far from Hernando. She helps a lot of people there.

Doesn't know too much about baseball—Claudia'll admit that—but she's learned some lessons I've taught her. Set your goal. Stay focused. And you'll succeed. I'm so damn proud of her, so very proud of her.

At the 1999 All-Star Game. I guess that was a hell of a show. That's Cal Ripken, Jr. in back of me. I gave Cal my Splendid Splinter Award after he broke Gehrig's record. By the way, did you know Lou Gehrig was in the very first game I played for Boston?

Helping me throw out the first pitch at the 1999 All-Star Game was Tony Gwynn,

who is not only a great hitter, but a wonderful, wonderful person. Gwynn hits for average. He hits in the clutch. Gwynn gets the bat on the ball. Doesn't go after bad pitches. Doesn't strike out. In 1994 he made a helluva run at .400, ended up at .394. He's a *student* of hitting. He works at it, thinks about, dreams hitting, goes over the videotapes, studies the pitchers.

My kind of hitter.

I'm always looking for good young hitters, smart young hitters. Boy, in 1997 I found one in Nomar Garciaparra. I saw him on TV. He looked like he knew what he was doing. I gave him a call. We talked hitting. I asked him questions, *lots of questions*, about hitting. You know, a lot of even the best god-

damn hitters don't know the answers. Nomar did. He impressed me and he's had a lot of success since, including a run at .400 in 2000.

Nomar, in fact, impressed me so much, that he is the reason we established the Ted Williams Rookie Award. I wanted some way to honor his performance, and it turned out that was the way and we've had the award ever since.

I've given a lot of advice to *hitters* over the years—and even to some pitchers. But there's not a helluva lot I can tell this fellow, Pedro Martinez. Oh, he's a good one, a great one, and

I'm so happy the Red Sox have got ahold of him. I faced some terrific, wonderful pitchers in my day, but this fellow is as good as any of them. He just proves how good the standard of play is today, and I'd hate to go against him.

W ell, what do you say about Hank Aaron? Seven hundred and fifty-five homers. Better than the Babe! More RBIs than Ruth too. More RBIs and total bases than anyone. How did he do it? He HIT! When Henry Aaron got his pitch he hit it. He didn't foul it off. He didn't watch it go by. He hit it. Henry Aaron—hitter!

Where do you start with Hank? I know where I started. I was just back from Korea and was in spring training in

Sarasota, and because I was an older, more experienced player, I got to play the first three innings and then BOOM! they take me out. I went in and showered and came on out because I wanted to watch the rest of the game. So I went out and just as I dove through the door, I hear WHACK!, and then the roar of the crowd—it was small but it made a helluva roar anyway—and one of my teammates said, "Did you see that guy hit that ball?" I didn't know who in the hell they were talking about—never heard of Hank Aaron before, I don't think— and he was rounding second. Boy did he hit that ball.

Aaron really wasn't very big then. He was thin then and still growing, I guess. He looked great for sure, but he hadn't hit any home runs and nobody knew too much about him.

Years later when I was managing the Senators, we had a couple of good young pitchers. One of them—Joe Coleman— was starting and he had good stuff, but I had to tell him, in some situations stuff is not enough. So anyway, Joe's starting this spring training game and Hank Aaron is in the Braves' starting lineup. So I took Coleman aside and I said, "You know today you're going to pitch against a great hitter." And I said, "Here's the way I want you to pitch to him. I want you to throw curveball, another curveball, another curveball, another curveball." Aaron finally grounded out to shortstop. Then I took him aside and said, "Now, the next time he gets up, you throw curveball, curveball." He did and he got two strikes real fast. And I had said, "When you get two strikes, I want you to throw the hardest, fastest, high fastball you can throw." And he did. The first one Aaron had seen. First time he had ever seen this guy. But he hit a ball that's still going on a line out of the ballpark. Boy, did he hit it! So we were convinced of one thing, he could hit a fastball, that's for damn sure. But he was a great hitter period, and an all-around great player. No question about it.

They named me to what they called the All-Century Team in 1999.

Had me to the World Series in Atlanta. Aaron. Musial. Mays. Spahn. Koufax. Berra. Bench. Schmidt. They were all there, and it was a helluva damn honor for *me* to be there, I tell you.

There were a lot of honors that year. That tremendous welcome they gave me at the All-Star Game at Fenway. That was wonderful, just so wonderful. I got a little misty. I admit it. Yes, I did.

When I was a kid, I would tell people, tell anybody who would listen, "All I want out of life is that, when I walk down the street, folks will say, 'There goes the greatest hitter who ever lived.'"

Maybe that seemed pretty far-fetched, to the people in San Diego. I don't know. Maybe it did. But I always *knew* I could make it happen. God, I worked so *damn* hard to *make* it happen. And when you see how people respect what you *did*, respect what you *are*—dammit, that makes it all worthwhile.

Would I do it all over again? Well, maybe I'd change a few things. Yes, maybe a few things. I could have handled some things better. I admit it. But I guess I'd still basically be Mr. Theodore Samuel Williams. Still be Teddy Ballgame. Still be me.

You bet I would.

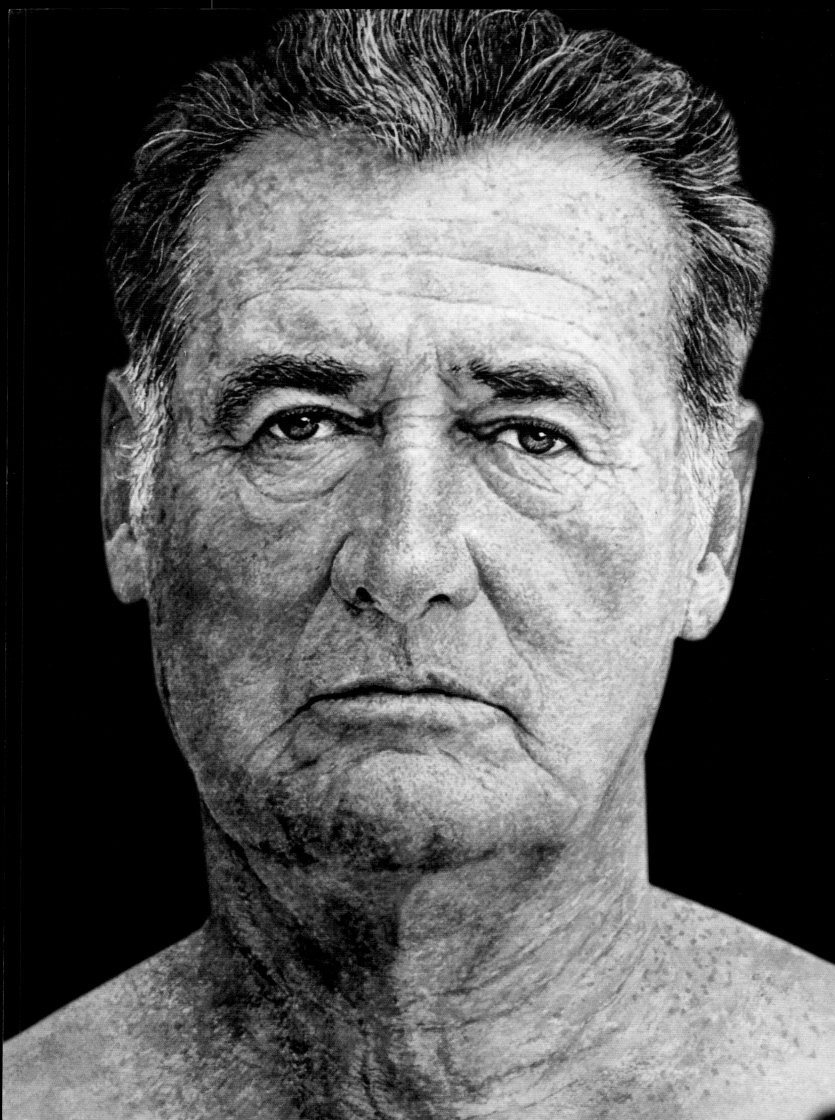

PHOTO CREDITS

Allsport: p. 195 (top)

Anonymous: p. 41

Associated Press: pp. 23, 42 (top), 43, 45, 53 (top left), 56, 57, 58 (bottom), 61, 66, 77, 79, 87, 88, 94, 95, 106, 121, 131 (bottom), 132, 136, 137, 158, 166 (bottom), 171 (top), 177, 178 (top), 179, 183 (top), 187, 189 (top), 191, 194, 199

AP/Wide World Photos: pp. 32, 36 (top), 86, 108, 122 (top), 134, 150, 161, 164

Bettmann/Corbis: pp. 150 (top), 151 (top), 159

Cleveland Public Library: pp. 52, 125, 156

Marshall Fogel: p. 36 (bottom)

F-Stop Fitzgerald, Inc.: pp. 176, 189 (bottom)

General Mills: p. 30 (bottom)

Arthur Griffin: pp. v, 28, 29, 31

Courtesy of Jimmy Fund: pp. 129 (top), 183 (bottom)

Armand LaMontagne: pp. 167, 200

Bill Loughman: pp. 8, 48, 49, 53 (top right), 76, 93 (top, right bottom), 114, 135, 151, 190 (top)

Ace Marchant: p. 148 (top)

Ray Medeiros: front end paper, pp. 20 (bottom), 21, 134 (bottom)

Monarch Company: p. 169 (bottom)

National Baseball Library: pp. 22, 24, 26, 33, 34-35, 42 (bottom), 50 (top), 78 (top), 84-85, 115, 118, 119 (top), 124, 146

J.J. Nissen Baking: p. 169 (top)

Bill Nowlin: p. 12

Collection of David Pietrusza: pp. 122 (bottom), 143, 174

Collection of Todd Radom: pp. 18 (left), 60 (bottom), 62 (top), 149 (chart), 157 (bottom), 171 (bottom), 195 (bottom)

Robert Riger: p. vi

Bob Rosato/Major League Baseball: p. 198

San Diego Hall of Champions: pp. 14 (top), 15, 17

Howard Snatchko: pp. 64-65

Sport: pp. 30, 74, 89, 90 (top), 202 (Calvin D. Campbell); 98, 116-117 (George Heyer); 155 (Bob Peterson); 2, 83, 126-127, 128 (Mort Schreiber); 152, 153 (George Woodruff)

Sports Illustrated: pp. 168 (Ozzie Sweet); 149 (John Zimmerman)

The Sporting News: pp. 5, 7, 9, 13, 25, 37, 38, 39 (left), 51, 53 (bottom), 63 (bottom), 92, 96, 113, 154, 166 (top)

John Thorn: pp. 133, 148 (middle)

George Tiedemann: pp 180, 181 bottom

TimePix: 172, 173 (top), 178 bottom, 186 (Bill Frakes); 90 bottom, 91, 105 (Leonard McCombe); 39, 44 (Gjon Mili); 97, 125 (Ralph Morse); 67 bottom, 72, 75, 100, 107, 108 (top), 131 (top) (Hy Peskin); 138 (Art Rickerby); 70, 120, 123 (Frank Scherschel); 71 (Joseph Scherschel); 104 (George Silk); 170 (Chuck Solomon); 139, 142 (Charles Trainor); 197

TimePix/SI: 197 (John Iacano); 109, back end paper (Richard Meek)

Transcendental Graphics: pp. 18 (right), 19, 40, 50 (bottom), 54, 55, 58 (top), 59, 63 (top), 68, 82, 102 (bottom), 110, 130, 148(bottom), 184

Unknown: pp. 69, 102 (top), 103, 112

Unknown Newspaper: pp. 20 (top), 27 (top)

UPI/Bettmann: pp 67 (top), 73, 111, 144, 145, 165, 190

Jay Walker: p. 10 (top)

Collection of Ted Williams Family Enterprises, Ltd: pp. 1, 6 (top), 10 (bottom), 11, 14 (bottom), 46, 47, 80, 81, 93 (bottom left), 101, 119 (bottom), 129 (bottom), 140 (top), 140 bottom, 141 (top left, top right), 141 bottom, 173 bottom, 175, 188, 192, 193, 196

Ted Williams League: p. 182

Ted Williams Museum and Hitters Hall of Fame: p. 175

Robert K. Wood: pp. 162, 163

Collection of Don Zimmer: p. 160

Ted Williams: My Life in Pictures was a team effort. Many individuals from Ted Williams Family Enterprises worked hard to make it a reality: John-Henry Williams, Anita Lovely, Eleanor Diamond, and Tom Sawyer, in particular. We are truly appreciative of their efforts. Claudia Williams and John Dutra also assisted in providing photography of Ted never before seen by the general public. John Kriston, executive director of the Ted Williams Museum and Hitters Hall of Fame, was invaluable in helping create the project.

Bill Nowlin, editor of the Ted Williams Museum's annual induction program, performed yeoman work not only in regard to image acquisition but also in the editorial process. Armand LaMontagne is not only a great artist but also a true gentleman, graciously providing us with images of Ted both young and old.

Irene Bayly and Cathy Karp helped our project along by researching microfilm regarding Ted's greatest games.

Total Sports Publishing acknowledges project editor Matthew Silverman, production coordinator Ann Sullivan, and designer Todd Radom. This book could not have been completed without the guiding hand of Rob Wilson and the efforts of Jed Thorn, Dianne Robinson, Donna Harris, Dave Weiner, and Wes Seeley.

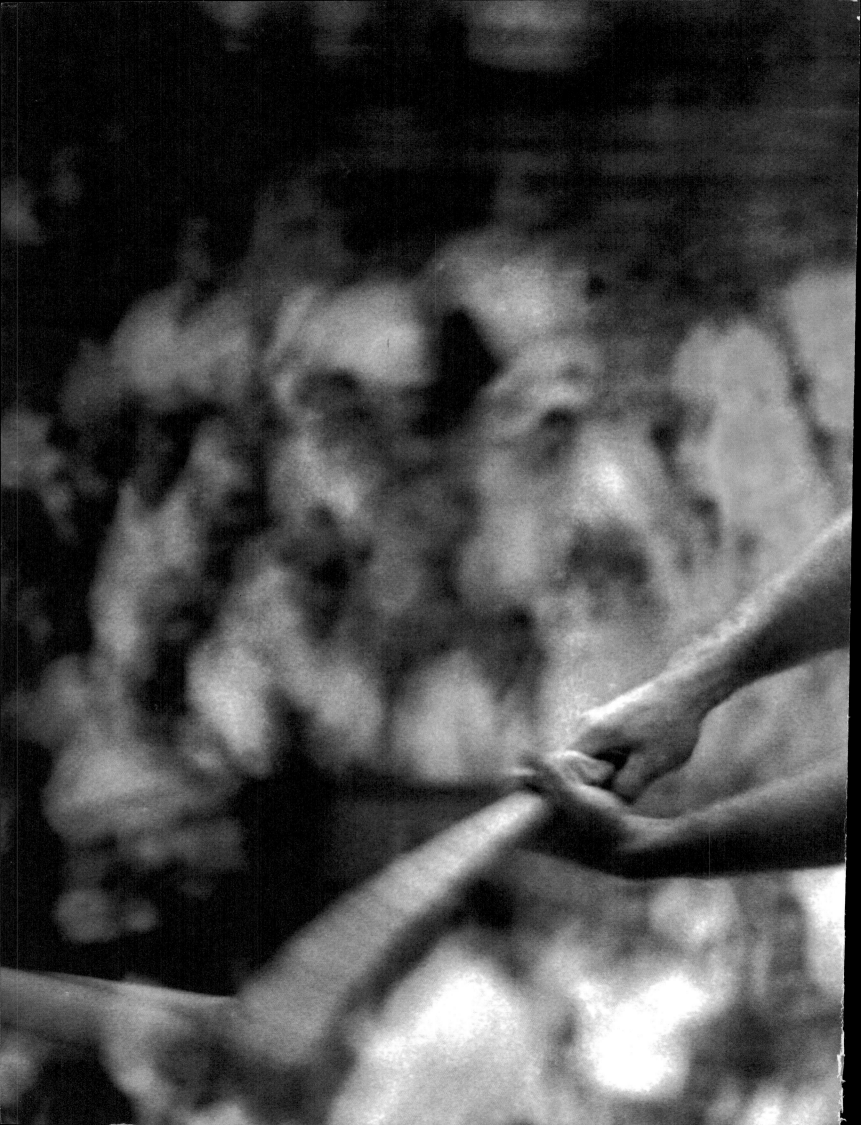